BOOKKEEPING MADE SIMPLE

David A. Flannery
Bryant & Stratton College
Associate Professor of Business
Director of Business and Accounting Programs

Edited by
Ned Cummings

Made Simple
BOOKS

A Made Simple Book
Broadway Books
New York

Produced by The Philip Lief Group, Inc.

For information, address: Broadway Books, a division of Random House, Inc., 1745 Broadway, New York, NY 10019.

Printed in the United States of America

Produced by The Philip Lief Group, Inc.
Managing Editors: Judy Linden, Jill Korot, Albry Montalbano.
Design: Annie Jeon.

Broadway Books titles may be purchased for business or promotional use or for special sales.
For information, please write to: Special Markets Department, Random House, Inc.
1745 Broadway, New York, NY 10019.

Visit our website at www.broadwaybooks.com.
First Broadway Books trade paperback edition published 2005.

Library of Congress Cataloging-in-Publication Data

Flannery, David A.
Bookkeeping made simple / David A. Flannery; edited by Ned Cummings.
p. cm.—(Made simple)
Rev. ed. of: Bookkeeping made simple / Louis W. Fields. Rev. ed., 1st ed. c1990.
Includes index.
ISBN 0-7679-1706-5
I. Cummings, Ned. II. Fields, Louis W. Bookkeeping made simple. III. Title.
IV. Series: Made simple (Broadway Books)

HF5635.F46 2005
657'.2—dc22 2004058600
10 9 8 7 6 5 4 3 2 1

DEDICATION

This book is dedicated to the memory of my stepfather, Dan. He lived his life as one should. Even when his body was infected with cancer, his spirit remained unaffected and positive. He was a constant source of inspiration for his family, friends, and coworkers. He taught me the importance of relationships, the value of life, and the virtue of love. Though it has been a long time since his passing, he remains an important model for my life.

ACKNOWLEDGMENTS

A task such as this cannot be completed alone. There are several people I want to thank for helping me with this project. First, thank you Ned Cummings for introducing me to this project and for your keen editorial assistance. Thank you Judy Linden, Jill Korot, and Albry Montalbano for giving me this opportunity, for your patience, and for your guidance on this endeavor. Also, I am very grateful for the quick and accurate typing work performed by Tiffany Sparks. Of course, none of this would have been possible without the support of my family. Thank you mom for working as hard as you did to provide my two beautiful sisters and me with the abilities to find opportunities where none existed. My children, David and Danielle, are a constant source of inspiration to me. Finally, I am forever in a debt of gratitude to my wife, Mary. She is my biggest fan and supports me in all of my endeavors. She has been kept awake many nights while I pecked away at the keyboard and graciously denies that she has been inconvenienced. She is a great woman, and I am very proud she is mine!

CONTENTS

INTRODUCTION

This revision of *Bookkeeping Made Simple* provides a new, updated look at the business of bookkeeping. You will be taking a journey through this often misunderstood, and sometimes feared, world of bookkeeping. Today, many of the functions of bookkeeping are accomplished with the use of a computer. Computer programs can help set up and track many different accounting and bookkeeping functions. The key word here is *help*. If you do not understand the basics, you will get very frustrated. Perhaps that is why you have this book right now. If this is the case, you are holding the right book. No matter what is advertised, computers do not keep books; people do. Those people are called bookkeepers. But what about an entrepreneur who wants to keep track of his or her own business records? This book is for you as well. The fact is that we are all bookkeepers to some extent. If you have been writing checks for more than a few months and haven't been jailed for passing bad checks, you have shown some bookkeeping ability. Where you may differ from a professional bookkeeper is how well you keep your books.

In the first several chapters, we will cover some of the fundamentals of bookkeeping: such topics as double-entry bookkeeping, the accounting equation, and the accounting cycle. In these chapters we will discuss how to document different transactions in the general journal, then post to specific account ledgers or special journals. Next, we will look at how to make sure everything we have done is correct by obtaining a trial balance. We will also learn how to prepare financial reports. Then we will see how to close the books in preparation for the next accounting period.

In Chapter 9, you will take a narrated walk through a simplified bookkeeping situation. Here you will be applying the lessons that you have learned in previous chapters. You will convert a fictitious business with a pile of receipts to one with an organized set of books and financial reports to present to the owners, so they know how their business is doing. While this may be a simplified scenario, it is not too different from what you could encounter. This may be the case whether you are hired to help someone else with his or her books or are working on books for your own business.

In the next several chapters, you will discover some specialized procedures. In these chapters you will be exposed to accounts used in merchandising or sales operations. You will also be introduced to concepts and terms such as *inventory, FIFO, LIFO, cost of goods sold,* and *depreciation*. Business checking accounts, petty cash funds, promissory notes, and interest will also be covered. Chapter 15 will provide information important to everyone: taking care of paychecks. Chapters 16 and 17 will explain the concept of partnerships and corporations, as well as how some things are recorded differently on financial statements.

In the final chapter, you will learn some of the terminology you may encounter when dealing with computers, as well as some of the different ways computers can assist in bookkeeping tasks. You will be led, step by step, through the creation of a simple spreadsheet program to account for expenses. This alone is a very valuable tool and one that can be adapted to suit many different uses.

This book was written to make bookkeeping simple and easy to understand. Whether you are a college student looking for a little help with accounting, an entrepreneur who wants to learn more about how to "keep books," or someone thinking of starting your own bookkeeping business, this is the right book for you. Bookkeeping is something that you will find in every business, no matter what the size of your company or field of work. Bookkeeping can help owners and management make better-informed decisions. These decisions can help prevent a business's failure or, even better, lead to growth and prosperity! And remember, that's the "bottom line."

CHAPTER 1

WHAT BOOKKEEPING IS ALL ABOUT

KEY TERMS

business, transaction, journal, account, T-account, debit, credit, balance sheet, income statement, asset, current assets, capital assets, owner's equity

I am sure you have heard that "The business of America is business." What is business? We might say that *business* consists of all commercial activities designed to sell goods and services to customers at a profit. Less formally, though, any enterprise in which we receive, spend, borrow, save, and (possibly) lend money is a business, whether it is a teenager's paper route, a drugstore, a computer repair shop, a manufacturing plant, or even a family. A professional practice like a doctor's office or a law firm is also a business in the sense we are using here. Additionally, nonprofit organizations such as charities, environmental groups, and religious organizations use bookkeeping to keep track of changes in the organization. Business is a game with many players, and bookkeepers keep the score.

In the past, business records were kept in big cloth-covered volumes: "the books." Today, the people who keep the records are still called bookkeepers. Progress in the field is demonstrated by the fact that they no longer use quill pens, and the "books" are most likely computer files. Whether you will be keeping books with pen and paper or on a computer, the principles you will use stay the same. What bookkeeping is all about is telling the owner(s) of a business (who might be you) how much money has come into the business, how much has gone out, what is owned, what is owed, and whether the business is gaining or losing in value.

Most bookkeepers use one of several readily available bookkeeping or accounting programs to "keep the books." The basic function of each of these programs is essentially the same. But to keep this book simple, we will first discuss how to keep the books manually. Keeping the books manually will allow us to become familiar with the terminology of bookkeeping. Once we understand the basics of bookkeeping, it will be a simple matter of applying that knowledge to the particular program we choose to use.

In this chapter you'll learn some basic terms and principles that you'll be using as long as you keep books. You'll be introduced to some bookkeeping "tools" that are more fully explained in later chapters. The physical form of these tools may change over time, but they are used for the same purposes by all businesses and are understood throughout the world of commerce. Essentially, bookkeepers use the same methods whether they are working for a sole proprietorship (owned by one person), a partnership, or a corporation. To keep things simple, we will describe bookkeeping operations in terms of a sole proprietorship. Chapter 16 contains a brief explanation of partnerships, and Chapter 17 discusses corporate bookkeeping.

KEEPING A RECORD OF TRANSACTIONS

A *transaction* is any business dealing that involves money. It may be a sale, a purchase, a loan, a lease payment, or any activity in which money is shifted from one "place" (account) to another. The money may be in the form of cash (currency), check, or money order, or it may be in the form of a promise to pay, such as a charge slip, a note, or a mortgage.

Numerous transactions occur in even the simplest of businesses. Let's look at some transactions that occur in a newspaper route. When your news carrier collects the fee from you or pays the newspaper company, each one of these is a transaction. And when the carrier pays the newspaper company, the newspaper pays its reporters and suppliers, and the suppliers in turn pay their workers and suppliers, each of these instances (and the many others that accompany them) is a transaction.

Your first responsibility as a bookkeeper is to keep a record of every transaction that occurs in the business. Unless you do this accurately, you cannot fulfill your responsibility of keeping score. A *journal* is the basic tool for recording all transactions chronologically (the order they occur) and is explained fully in Chapter 3. Making a *journal entry* is the process of recording in the journal transactions that have occurred and is more formally called *journalizing*. Later, the journal entries are transferred to a various number of records called accounts that are used to prepare many kinds of financial reports. An *account* is the place to which journal entries are transferred and recorded. *Posting* is the process of transferring information from journal entries to accounts.

The title of the account is listed above two columns. This shape resembles a capital "T," thus these accounts are called "T-accounts." A *T-account* represents a ledger account and is used to help show the effects of one or more transactions. A bookkeeping entry is either a debit or a credit. A *debit* is always entered in the left-hand column of a T-account. A *credit* is always entered in the right-hand column of a T-account. (See Figure 1.1.) Although people often assume that a debit means a subtraction and a credit means an addition, this is not necessarily the case. There are rules that determine whether something is a debit or a credit; these rules pertain in part to what is called the "normal account balance." The normal account balance will be described in detail in Chapter 3. Don't worry if all of these rules do not make sense to you, especially at first. You will see a theme of repetition and application that will make the process of learning this material simple.

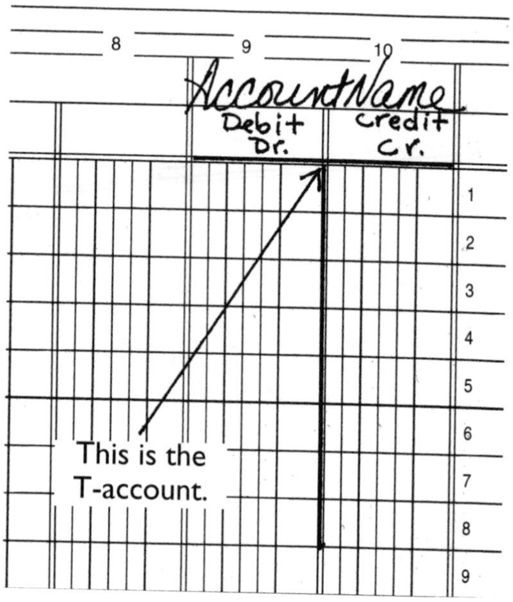

Figure 1.1

As you'll see, the basic principle behind double-entry bookkeeping, the kind you are learning, is that debits and credits must always balance (equal each other). This means that *an item that is credited in one place must be debited somewhere else.* Every transaction eventually involves both a credit and a debit. Beginning bookkeepers often are confused whether to debit or credit an item but understanding this problem is what much of this book is about.

THE SECRET OF RITA'S LOCKED DRAWER

Rita had been keeping the books for fifty years. "She knows everything there is to know," the others told newcomers. "The boss depends on her." Rita was a creature of habit. Every morning she would pour herself a cup of tea. Then, before settling down to work, she would look over her shoulder to make sure no one was close by before opening the first left-hand drawer of her desk a few inches and peering inside. Then she would shut and lock it. One night, Rita died in her sleep. Her curious colleagues opened the locked drawer to clean it out. They found it empty except for a yellowed slip of paper pasted to the bottom. It read:

DEBITS GO ON THE LEFT; CREDITS GO ON THE RIGHT

After your journal entries have been posted to various accounts, you will be able to prepare financial statements to summarize the condition of the business. Is the business making a profit or operating at a loss? Are the owners increasing their investment, or is the business losing value? We will talk more about the meaning of these questions in later chapters. For now, you need to know the purpose of two kinds of financial statements, the balance sheet and the income statement.

The *balance sheet* shows what the business owns (*assets*), what it owes (*liabilities*), and what the current value of the company is for its owners. The balance sheet provides a snapshot of the value of a business at a particular point in time. The *income statement* (sometimes called a *profit and loss statement* or *P&L*) lists income over a specified period of time, such as a year or a calendar quarter, and subtracts expenses over the same period to show whether a profit was earned or a loss incurred for that time frame.

ASSETS: WHAT THE BUSINESS OWNS

An *asset* is any property the business owns and any claim it has on the property of others. Remember that you list any business property as an asset, regardless of whether it is fully paid for. Any amount owed on the property will be listed as a liability (see next section). Assets include such things as:

- Land
- Buildings
- Equipment
- Cash
- Accounts receivable
- Inventories
- Materials

Any item of value to the business is an asset. When an asset is acquired, you record the dollar amount paid for it, for example, "Ford delivery van, $36,500."

How Are Assets Classified?

The two main kinds of assets are current assets and capital assets. *Inventory* (stocks of goods to be sold) and materials (stocks of raw materials or components) are current assets. Current assets continually change. A *current asset* is cash or items that will become cash in the foreseeable future because they are intended for sale or items the business will consume within one year. They are listed on the balance sheet in order of their liquidity. *Liquidity* is the speed with which an asset can be turned into cash. Cash (on hand or in a demand deposit in the bank) is therefore listed first. Cash is the first resource for paying bills. *Accounts receivable* is the money owed by customers of the business for goods or services they have purchased on credit. It is listed next because it is assumed they will soon become cash. Inventories (goods held for sale) are listed next, then supplies and prepaid items such as insurance and rent paid in advance.

A *capital asset* is a permanent item used directly or indirectly to produce the product or service that the business sells—for example, a building, equipment, a truck, or a computer. In the lists that follow current assets and capital assets are defined. Note the order in which they appear in standard bookkeeping practice.

Current Assets

Cash: The total of currency (dollars), coins, money orders, checks, back drafts, and letters of credit the firm has on hand or in bank accounts from which the money can be drawn immediately (demand deposits).

Accounts Receivable: Amount owed by customers who purchased goods and services for which they have not yet paid.

Inventories: Dollar value in actual cost of goods a firm has for sale (that is, its stock).

Supplies: Materials used in conducting the daily operations of the business, such as stationery, computer disks, printer cartridges (office supplies) or lubricating oil, paint, solder (factory materials).

Prepaid Items: Amounts already paid for services the business has yet to receive—for example, insurance.

To summarize, *current assets* are comprised of (1) cash or items that will become cash in the foreseeable future because they are intended for sale and (2) items that the business will consume within a year.

Capital Assets

Land: Value of acreage owned by the business at actual purchase price.

Buildings: Purchase price or construction cost of structures, including surveys, architect fees, engineering fees, permits, etc.

Equipment: Itemized list of the price paid for machines, vehicles, boilers, conveyors, shelving, and durable tools, as well as office equipment, computers, desks, and other furniture. The value of equipment is subject to depreciation (see Chapter 11).

Note that whether an item is listed as a current asset or a capital asset depends on its intended purpose. If you had an appliance business, you would list air conditioners held for sale as current assets, but an air conditioner installed to keep the store cool would be a capital asset. The deciding factor in determining whether something is a capital asset is whether it will be retained for use within the business at some time.

EQUITIES: WHAT THE BUSINESS OWES ITSELF AND OTHERS

An *equity* is any debt a business owes. There are two types of equity—creditors and owner's equity. Creditor's equity is more commonly known as liabilities, the term we will use throughout the book. *Liabilities* are legal claims against the business by persons or corporations other than the owners. These claims come before the rights of the owners. They may consist of money owed to suppliers or vendors for inventory or supplies, or to banks or loan companies for equipment, money owed for taxes, and so on. *Owner's equity* is the amount left over after all liabilities have been deducted from assets; this is the portion of the assets belonging to the owners of the business; it is sometimes called *capital* or *net worth*.

How Are Liabilities Classified?

Like assets, liabilities are classified as being short-term or long-term. *Current liabilities* are like current assets; *long-term liabilities* are like capital assets. Generally, liabilities are considered current if they must be paid within the current accounting year.

Liabilities are listed in the following order.

Current Liabilities

Accounts Payable: Bills owed to creditors such as vendors or suppliers.

Wages Payable: Payroll due.

Short-Term Notes Payable: Borrowing that must be repaid within the current accounting year.

Long-Term Liabilities

Long-Term Notes Payable: Borrowing to be repaid after one year.

Mortgages Payable: Balance due on business mortgages.

With these basic terms in mind, you are ready to address what is called the "accounting equation" and the basic functions of bookkeeping in Chapter 2.

SUMMARY

All organizations that deal with money or other assets use some form of bookkeeping. They need to keep records of their transactions or changes in the organization. This is accomplished by recording these transactions in journals. Information recorded in the journals will later be posted to ledger accounts that will keep track of a specific type or family of transactions. These are known as accounts. All information recorded in the journal or ledger accounts is assigned a side of the account, debit for the left side or credit for the right side. Every entry is recorded in two different accounts, also known as double-entry bookkeeping. Anything that is debited in one account must be credited in another account.

An asset is something that the business owns. There are different classifications of assets based on how the asset is used. An asset that is or will soon become cash is considered a current asset. An asset that is permanent, used to operate the business, or will not be converted to cash in the next year is generally considered a capital asset. Equity is something that the business owes to outsiders or to the owners. This is broken into two types of equity: (1) liabilities, something the business owes to outside interest, and (2) owner's equity, what the business owes to the owner(s).

CHAPTER 2

THE BOOKKEEPING EQUATIONS

KEY TERMS

initial capital, revenues, expenses, net income

The most basic principle of bookkeeping is that what is owned must always balance what is owed. This can be expressed as the "accounting equation."

THE ACCOUNTING EQUATION

$A = E$

Assets = Equities

The fundamental accounting equation is often abbreviated to *A* = *E*. It means that assets must equal equities. Equities are made up of two categories, liabilities (creditors' equity) and owner's equity. Capitalism, the economic system of the United States, takes its name from the fact that the equity of U.S. business enterprises belongs to private individuals, singly or in voluntarily formed groups. Another way to express this equation is to separate the two major categories of equity. You will find that owner's equity will normally be represented by an "E" (for equity), liabilities with a "L," and assets with an "A." Thus the equation can be expressed as follows:

$$A = L + E$$

This is the universally known accounting equation and is one of the keys to understanding the field of bookkeeping.

> The term "capitalism" was originally coined by Karl Marx, the founder of communism. He noted that business owners have an almost insatiable desire to accumulate wealth. The term was originally associated with greed and cruelty. The definition has changed over the years, as it now describes an economic system where the majority of businesses and services are privately owned and controlled.

Let's look at something that most of us understand. Let's say that you bought a $25,000 car and gave the dealer $5,000 in cash or trade and borrowed the rest from the bank ($20,000). You would have a $25,000 car and owe $20,000 to the bank. To the bookkeeper, you would have an asset valued at $25,000 and subtract the liability of $20,000 (a creditor's equity—the bank) to arrive at the owner's equity of $5,000. Your balance sheet would then be:

$25,000 = $20,000 + $5,000
(ASSETS) = (LIABILITY) + (EQUITY)
$A = L + E$

A precise bookkeeper will frequently check to verify that "A" does indeed equal "L" plus "E." If it does not, an error has been made somewhere and the books are not in balance.

THE BALANCE SHEET

When all the assets, liabilities, and owner's equity have been totaled, they are summarized on a balance sheet. Assets are listed by categories on the left side and equities (liabilities and owner's equity) on the right. The sum on the left side must equal, or balance, the sum on the right. Figure 2.1 shows a typical balance sheet.

Among the assets of the business is the initial capital invested into the business by its owner(s). *Initial capital* is money or other assets that the owner puts into the business to meet start-up expenses and keep the business going until money from customers begins to come in. You may put a truck or van that belongs to you into the business's name. These become part of the owners' equity.

How would a bookkeeper handle such a transaction? Remember that $A = L + E$.

My New Company, Inc.
Balance Sheet
Dec. 31, 20__

Assets			Liabilities		
Current Assets			**Current Liabilities**		
Cash	______		Accounts Payable		______
Accounts Receivable	______		Wages Payable		______
Inventory	______		Total Current Liabilities		______
Supplies	______				
Prepaid Insurance	______				
Total Current Assets		______			
Capital Assets			**Long-Term Liabilities**		
Truck	______		Mortgage	______	
Equipment	______		Total Long-Term Liabilities		______
Total Capital Assets		______			
			Total Liabilities		______
			Owner's Equity		
					______
Total Assets		______	Total Liabilities And Owner's Equity		______

Figure 2.1

Suppose you put up $20,000 in cash to start your garden supply business. The transaction would increase your cash on hand (an asset) by $20,000. But it would also increase your owner's equity by $20,000. Thus,

$A = L + E$
$20,000 cash = $0 + $20,000 equity

Next, suppose your business purchases $5,000 worth of garden equipment for resale. This transaction would be recorded as follows:

Assets	=	Liabilities	+	Equity
$20,000	=	$0	+	$20,000
– 5,000 (cash)				
+ 5,000 (inventory)				
$20,000	=	$0	+	$20,000

The purchase reduced your cash on hand (an asset) by $5,000, but it increased your inventory (also an asset) by $5,000. Both sides of the equation still balance.

To deliver your garden equipment, you now decide to purchase a truck costing $35,000. You put down $3,000 from your business's cash account and sign a note, or equipment loan, for $32,000. Now your account looks like this:

Assets	=	Liabilities	+	Equity
$20,000	=	$0	+	$20,000
– 5,000 (cash)				
+ 5,000 (inventory)				
$20,000		$0	+	$20,000
+ 35,000 (truck)				
– 3,000 (cash)		32,000 (note)		
$52,000	=	$32,000	+	$20,000

When you add all the columns, you will find that one side still equals the other side. (See Figure 2.2.)

Now let's look at another transaction. Suppose you sell $2,500 of the garden equipment for $3,250. This transaction reduces your inventory (assets) by $2,500 and increases your cash on hand (assets) by $3,250. Does this unbalance your accounts? No, because $750 of the amount received for the garden equipment is profit; it is added to your owner's equity (see Figure 2.2.) Your accounts now read:

Assets = Liabilities + Equity
$52,750 = $32,000 + $20,750

The Balance Sheet Equation

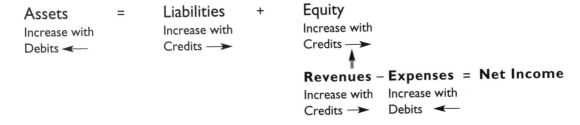

Assets = Liabilities + Equity

Assets: Increase with Debits ←
Liabilities: Increase with Credits →
Equity: Increase with Credits →
↑
Revenues – Expenses = Net Income

Revenues: Increase with Credits →
Expenses: Increase with Debits ←

Figure 2.2

Of course, these are simplified examples, and the real transactions you will be working with as a bookkeeper can be more complicated. For now, however, practice keeping your accounts in balance by continuing with your hypothetical garden equipment business:

- You sell $1,200 more garden equipment "on account" (that is, your customer has not paid for them).
- You make a $1,000 payment on the truck loan.

Can you see how each of these transactions affects your *A* = *L* + *E* equation? Have you kept the equation in balance?

Take a moment to review the Balance Sheet Equation. (See Figure 2.2.)

Review Figure 2.3 to see the breakdown of these transactions.

THE NET INCOME FORMULA

In addition to handling assets and equity, bookkeepers must work with revenues and expenses. *Revenues* are the earnings of the business—the money that comes in from the sale of products (sales revenue) or services (service revenue). You earn sales revenue by selling goods from inventory and service revenue from selling time and talent. Many

Rundown of Garden Equipment Business Transactions

Assets	=	Liabilities	+	Capital
$20,000	=	$0	+	$20,000
– 5,000 (cash)				
+ 5,000 (equipment)				
$20,000		$0	+	$20,000
+35,000 (truck)				
– 3,000 (cash)		+ 32,000 (note)		
$52,000	=	$32,000	+	$20,000
– 2,500 (inventory)				
+ 3,250 (cash)				+ 750 (profit)
$52,750	=	$32,000	+	$20,750
– 1,200 (inventory)				
+ 1,200 (accounts receivable)				
$52,750	=	$32,000	+	$20,750
– 1,000 (cash)		– 1,000 (note)		
$51,750	=	$31,000	+	$20,750

Figure 2.3

businesses earn both kinds of revenue. For example, an electronics store earns sales revenue each time a television set or DVD player is sold. It earns service revenue through repairs and, perhaps, through DVD rentals. Revenues are an inflow of assets, whether they are in the form of cash or in the form of accounts receivable.

Conversely, *expenses* are the outflow of assets and are the cost of doing business. To use the electronics store example again, TV sets purchased for resale, the rent for the store, the decorative displays, the sales slips, and the salary and commission of the salespeople are all expenses. Expenses may flow out in the form of cash or by incurring accounts payable (credit).

Net income is what remains after all expenses are subtracted from revenues. You might casually refer to this as profit, but profit takes a number of forms: gross profit and net profit, sometime referred to as profit before taxes and profit after taxes. Net income is what is left after all expenses have been met. You have heard it called "the bottom line" because that is where it appears on the accounting page. Expressed as a formula, the final calculation of net income (NI) looks like this:

$$R - E = NI$$

(Revenues) − (Expenses) = (Net income)

THE INCOME STATEMENT

Revenues, expenses, and net income are summarized on a statement called an income statement. An income statement reveals all revenues earned and expenses incurred by a business during a specified period of time: a month, a quarter (three months), six months, or a year. If the yearly period used is from January 1 through December 31, it is called a calendar year. If some other 365-day

A Cut Above Beauty Salon
Income Statement
For the year ending 12/31/20__

Revenues		
Sales Revenue	$180,000	
Service Revenue	205,000	
Total Revenues		$385,000
Expenses		
Wages	$85,000	
Rent	120,000	
Insurance	52,000	
Taxes	70,000	
Advertising	15,000	
Telephone	2,400	
Total Expenses		$344,400
Net Income		$40,600

Figure 2.4

period is used (for example, a year calculated from the date the business opened), it is called a fiscal year. "Fiscal" means financial.

Figure 2.4 shows a typical income statement. Some people call this a statement of income and expense or a profit and loss statement, but income statement is the term most often used by professionals. Pay particular attention to the location of dollar signs, the location of the columns, and the single and double underscoring. Dollar signs appear next to the top number in every column and at every total. A column total shifts to the right when it is to be used in further addition or subtraction. Underscoring appears below every subtotal, and double underscoring appears beneath the final amount.

Keeping the records of income and expenses and translating them into income statements and balance sheets are the basic functions of all bookkeeping, whether the business is a multimillion dollar corporation or a small start-up firm.

SUMMARY

Two key elements of bookkeeping and accounting are the balance sheet and the income statement. The balance sheet operates on the premise of the accounting equation, which states that what the business owns must equal what it owes. In other words, assets equal equities. The balance sheet places all items that are assets on the left side of the sheet and all liabilities and owner's equity on the right side of the sheet. The two sides must be in balance or else there is an error that must be uncovered.

Net income is what remains after all expenses have been subtracted from total revenue. It is also known as the bottom line. The income statement is the report used to determine the profit of a company for a particular period of time, usually a year.

EXERCISES

2.1 Using the worksheet in Figure 2.5, prepare a balance sheet using the following information for the Jones Company on June 30, 20__.

Cash	$2,200
Inventory	2,100
Prepaid rent	2,500
Store equipment	1,700
Computer	1,900
Accounts payable	750
Sixty-day bank note	2,100
Accounts receivable	4,200
Three-year bank note	2,100
Owner's equity	4,500

2.2 Identify each of the following as an asset, a liability, or an owner's equity.
1. Cash
2. Accounts payable
3. Interest due to bank
4. Supplies on hand
5. Land and building
6. Insurance paid in advance

2.3 Create an Income Statement for A Cut Above Beauty Salon using the following information: From January 1 through March 31 the owner deposited $50,000 for cutting and blow-drying hair and $25,000 for selling hair spray and conditioners. The rent for the quarter was $6,000, electricity $1,000, wages $23,000, and insurance $900. Use Figure 2.6 to record your answer.

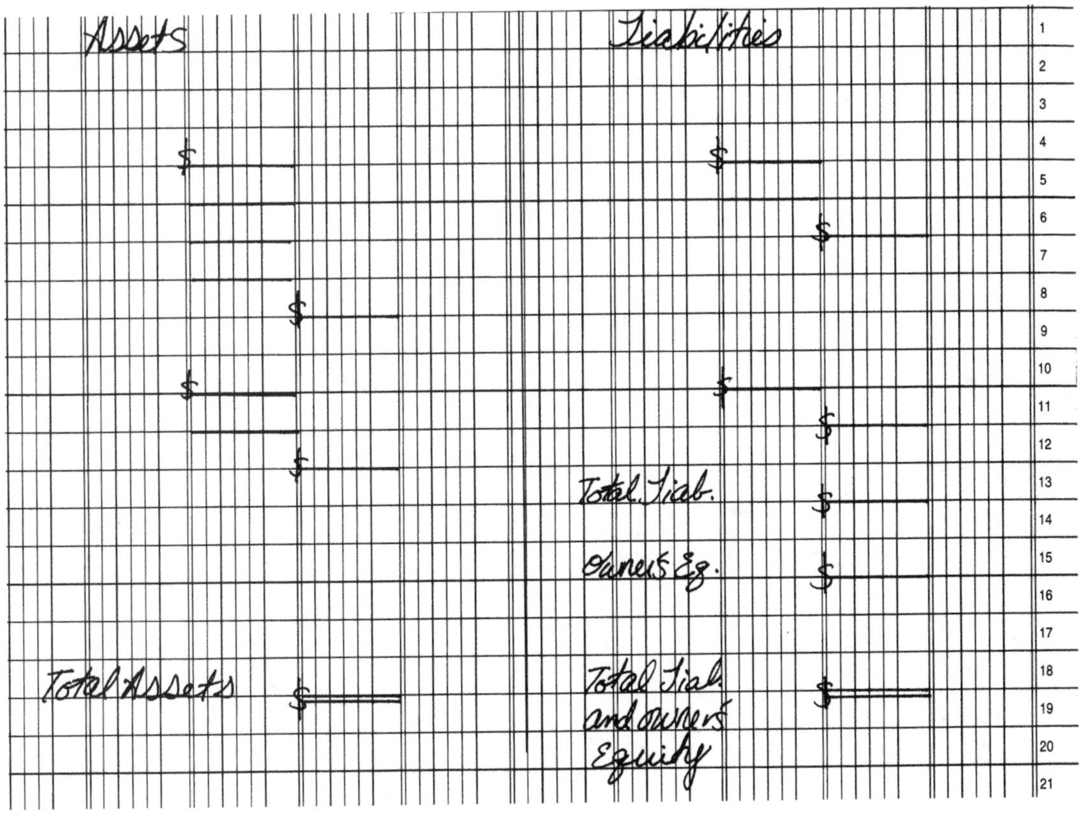

Figure 2.5

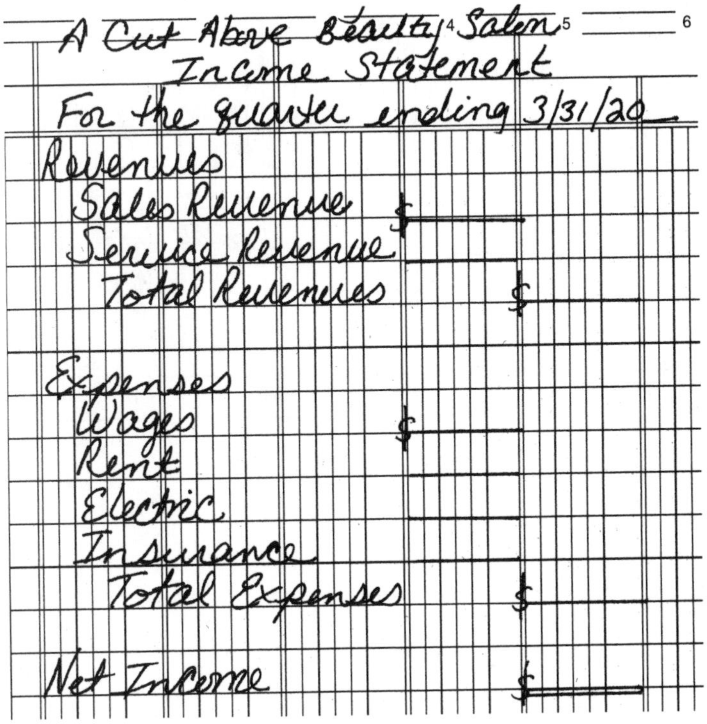

Figure 2.6

ANSWERS

2.1 See Figure 2.5A

2.2 1. Cash—Asset

2. Accounts Payable—Liability

3. Interest due to bank—Liability

4. Supplies on hand—Asset

5. Land and building—Asset

6. Insurance paid in advance—Asset

2.3 See Figure 2.6A

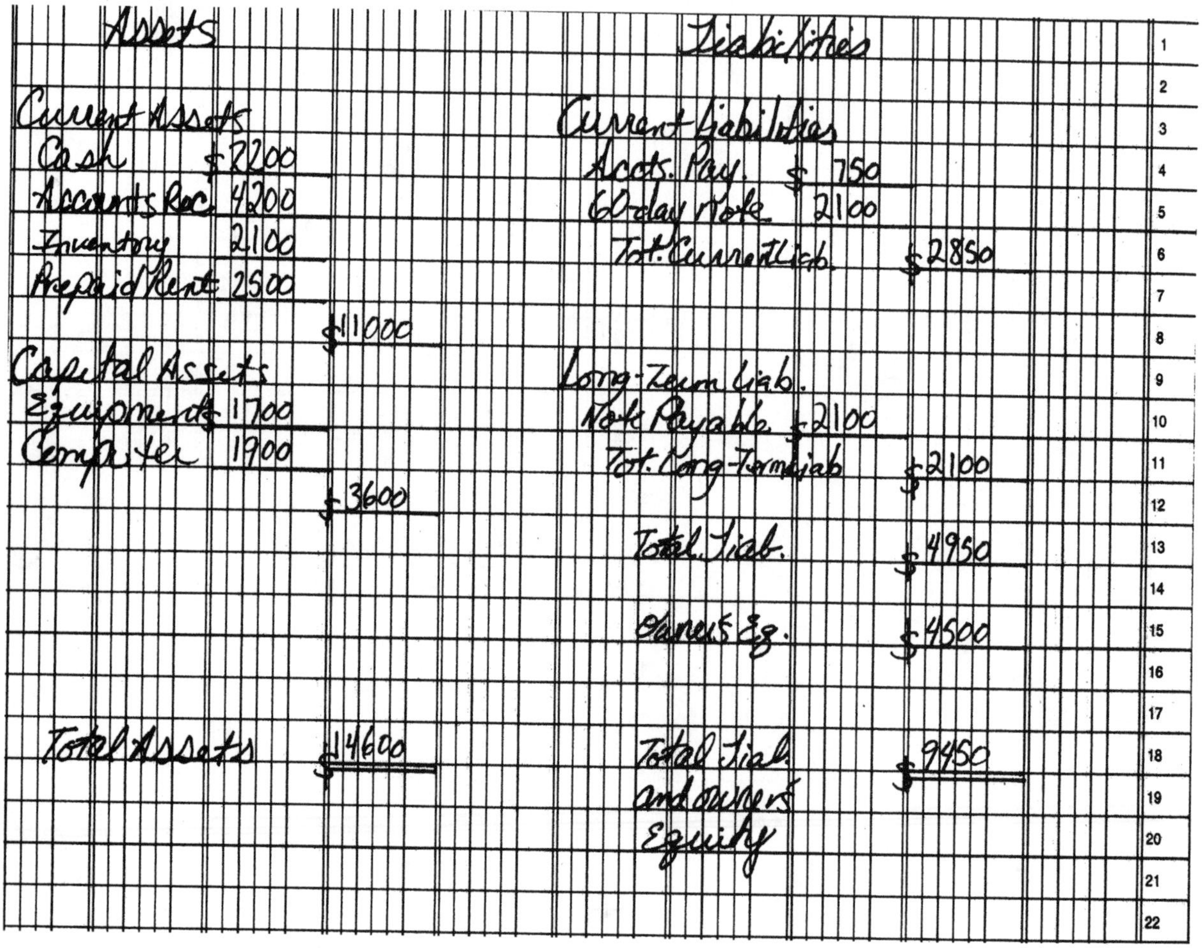

Figure 2.5A

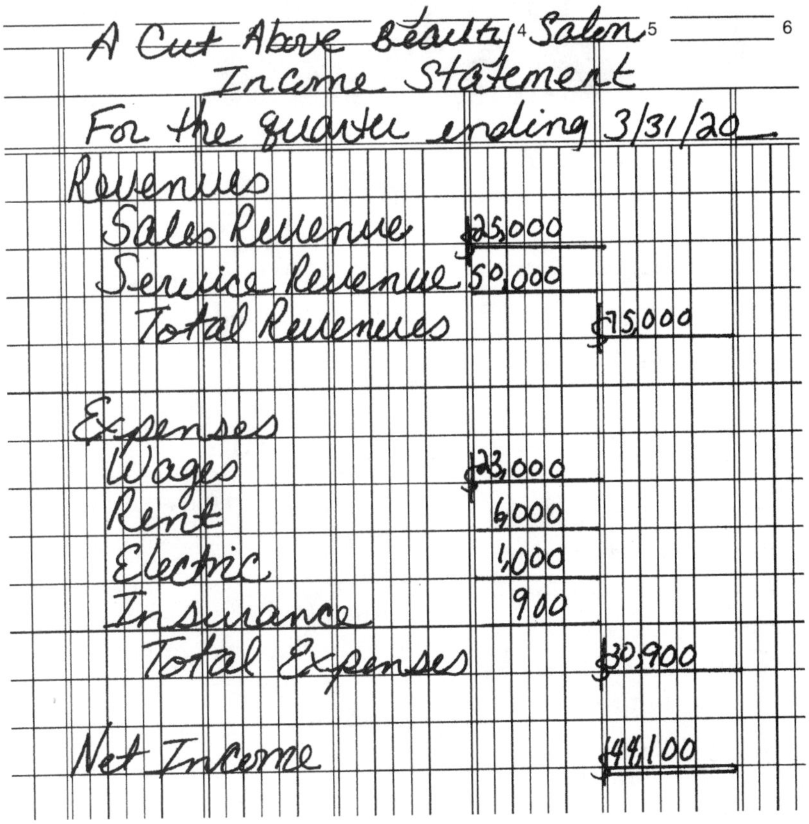

A Cut Above Beauty Salon
Income Statement
For the quarter ending 3/31/20__

Revenues		
Sales Revenue	$25,000	
Service Revenue	50,000	
Total Revenues		$75,000
Expenses		
Wages	$23,000	
Rent	6,000	
Electric	1,000	
Insurance	900	
Total Expenses		$30,900
Net Income		$44,100

Figure 2.6A

CHAPTER 3 THE JOURNAL

KEY TERMS

journalizing, posting, entry, double-entry system, trial balance, normal account balance, compound entries

You may have noticed that some information from your earlier reading is being repeated. This is intentional! Repetition will help you learn the language of bookkeeping. The procedures you will be learning in Chapters 3 through 8 are stages in the accounting cycle. Picture the cycle as a circle that repeats itself again and again throughout the life of the business, just as the seasons repeat themselves each year and we revisit topics in this book.

THE ACCOUNTING CYCLE

The cycle begins when a transaction occurs. Journalizing is the practice whereby every time a transaction is made, it is recorded. Each transaction brings about a change in one or more accounts: assets, liabilities, owner's equity, revenues, or expenses. Your accounts must be verified for accuracy. At least once each business year, you will prepare a work sheet so that you can summarize these changes in balance sheets and operating statements. Many businesses will do this quarterly. You must make adjustments and entries for changes that are not supported by documents, such as receipts or invoices. Then, you will "close the books" in preparation for the beginning of the next cycle. (See Figure 3.1.)

THE JOURNAL

The *general journal* is the daily "diary" in which each transaction is recorded, or entered, and is also known simply as the journal. In the journal, transactions are listed in chronological order—that is, in the order of their date of occurrence. The *book of original entry* (yet another name for the journal) is the starting place for all bookkeeping.

THE DOUBLE-ENTRY SYSTEM

In keeping your journal, you work with written records or documents such as vendors' invoices, customers' sales slips, records of charges, shipping papers (bills of lading), bank deposit records, and so on. Each time you make such a record, you are making an entry. *Entry* is the term used to describe the recording of a transaction. The *double-entry system* is where each transaction is recorded twice: as a debit to one account and as a credit to another. In order for the "books" to be "in balance," the total of debits in all accounts must equal the total of credits in all accounts. If they do not, you know immediately that an error has been made; an entry was omitted or made incorrectly. *Thus, the double-entry system provides a continuous check on accuracy.*

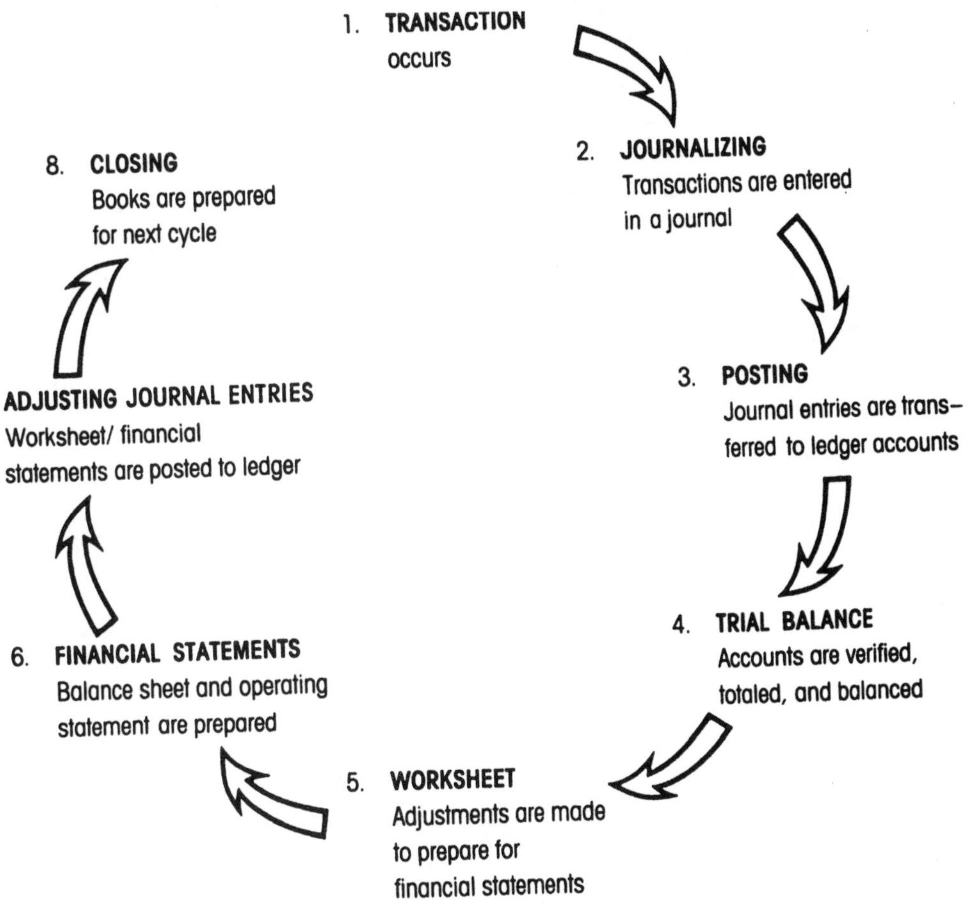
1. TRANSACTION
occurs
2. JOURNALIZING
Transactions are entered
in a journal
3. POSTING
Journal entries are transferred to ledger accounts
4. TRIAL BALANCE
Accounts are verified,
totaled, and balanced
5. WORKSHEET
Adjustments are made
to prepare for
financial statements
6. FINANCIAL STATEMENTS
Balance sheet and operating
statement are prepared
ADJUSTING JOURNAL ENTRIES
Worksheet/ financial
statements are posted to ledger
8. CLOSING
Books are prepared
for next cycle

Figure 3.1—Accounting Cycle

MAKING JOURNAL ENTRIES

To begin your journal, you "head up" a two-column journal page or sheet with the name of the business and the words "General Journal." The left-hand column is headed "Dr." (the abbreviation for debit) and the right-hand column "Cr." (the abbreviation for credit). Since the column dividers resemble the letter "T," this arrangement is called a T-account; we first saw this in Chapter 1. On the far left is a column for the date. Figure 3.2 shows a journal page prepared to accept entries.

Note that journal entries are not totaled. The data from these entries is totaled when a trial balance is taken, at which time the totals are transferred to the income statement and the balance sheet (see Chapter 7). A *trial balance* is a list of all accounts and their balances at a specific point in time.

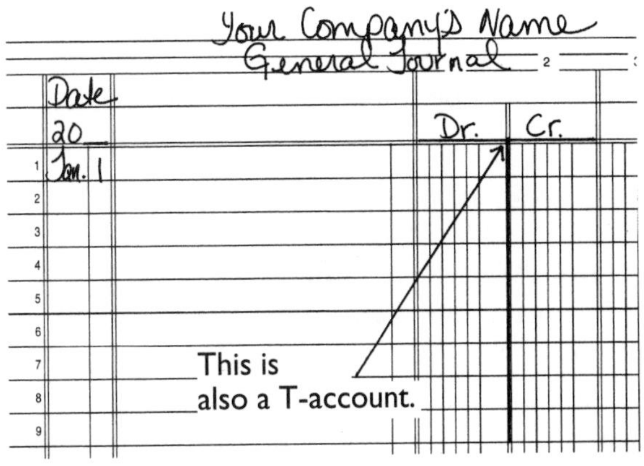
Your Company's Name
General Journal
Date
20
Jan. 1
Dr.
Cr.
This is
also a T-account.

Figure 3.2

Debit or Credit?

Now you are ready to enter transactions. Before you can begin, though, you need to know whether a given transaction should be entered in the debit (Dr.) column or in the credit (Cr.) column. Every entry you make in the journal will eventually be posted to a ledger account. Doing this is discussed in Chapter 4 but to make the journal entry, you need to know whether a debit or a credit increases or decreases the kind of account it applies to. Memorize these rules:

- Assets *increase* with debits and *decrease* with credits.
- Expenses *increase* with debits and *decrease* with credits.
- Liabilities (creditors' equity) *increase* with credits and *decrease* with debits.
- Owner's equity *increases* with credits and *decreases* with debits.
- Revenues *increase* with credits and *decrease* with debits.

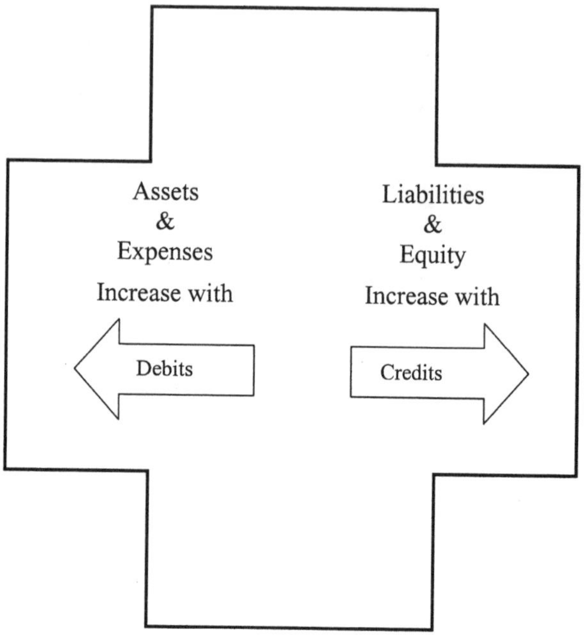

Figure 3.3

Keep Figure 3.3 in front of you until you become perfectly acquainted with the rules for using debits and credits in making journal entries. Note that if the figure had used a minus sign (to signify decreases), each of the items would be listed on the opposite side.

Normal Account Balances

In any given account, increases will exceed decreases under normal circumstances. For example, a cash account would normally have a positive total rather than a negative one. Increases to assets will ordinarily exceed decreases (unless the business is losing money). You can see that having a balance of –$80 in the cash account would be awkward. So would having a minus (credit) balance in the land or building accounts. Thus, a *normal account balance* is the side of the account (debit or credit) where increases are recorded. If an account is even, record a zero on the side of an account's normal account balance.

Table 3.1 shows the "Normal Account Balance" for each category of account, as well as how to treat a transaction. Since revenues customarily grow, the normal balance in that account is a credit. Expenses also grow, so the normal balance is a debit. A balance that is out of normal circumstance may signal an error.

Each time bookkeepers enter a transaction in the journal, they must go through the following thinking process:

1. What accounts are affected by this entry? (Note that more than one account is affected.)

Table of Debits & Credits Showing Normal Account Balances			
Category of Account	If the transaction increases the account enter a...	If the transaction decreases the account enter a...	The normal balance is a...
Asset	Debit	Credit	Debit
Liability	Credit	Debit	Credit
Owner's Equity	Credit	Debit	Credit
Revenue	Credit	Debit	Credit
Expense	Debit	Credit	Debit

Table 3.1

2. Are these accounts assets, liabilities, owner's equity, revenues, or expenses?

3. Does the transaction increase or decrease them?

4. Does this information call for a debit entry or a credit entry?

For example: The cash sales for this week were $8,000. You need to enter this transaction in the journal. To decide which accounts are affected, you use the following thought process: "I know that the event involves cash sales. I know cash is an asset and sales is a revenue. I see that cash (an asset) increased and sales (a revenue) also increased. An increase in an asset calls for a debit, while an increase in a revenue calls for a credit." Your journal entry would look like Figure 3.4. You can get additional practice with Exercise 3.1 at the end of this chapter.

TO CREDIT OR TO DEBIT?

Now, review what you have learned by considering whether you would use a debit or a credit journal entry to show the following:

- An increase in cash
- A decrease in inventory
- An increase in machinery
- The spending of cash
- Going into debt (increasing a liability)
- Paying a bill that is due
- Earning revenue from a sale
- Increasing your (the owner's) equity

You can double-check your answers at the end of the chapter.

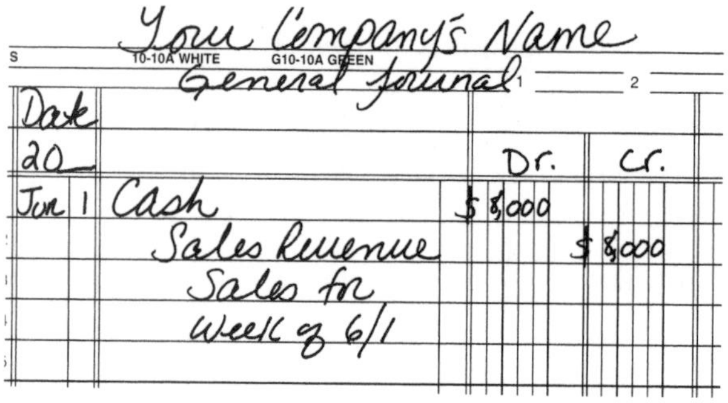

Figure 3.4

Compound Entries

Compound entries are used when a transaction affects more than two accounts. For example, suppose your business purchased a $36,000 truck for $7,000 down and signed a note payable for $29,000. In this case two lines are used to record the two credits. The total of the credits should equal the total of the debits. This transaction is shown in Figure 3.5.

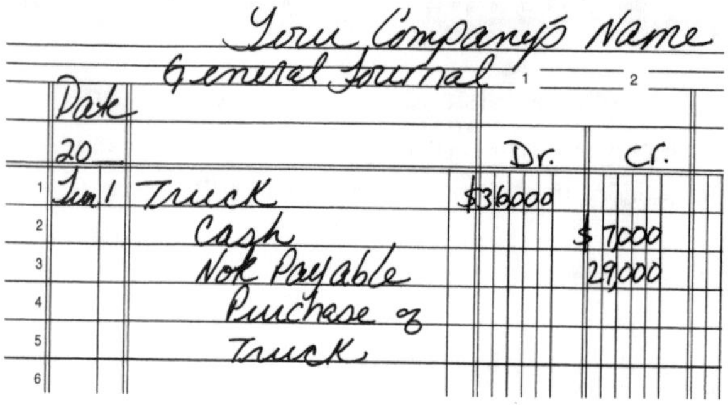

Figure 3.5

Journal Entries for Revenues and Expenses

Revenue, such as the income from the sales of goods or services, adds to the owner's equity account. For this reason, the revenue account is increased with credit. (See Figure 3.6.)

Conversely, expenses increase with debits and serve to reduce the owner's equity account. A helpful guideline is to remember that expenses are almost always debited. The

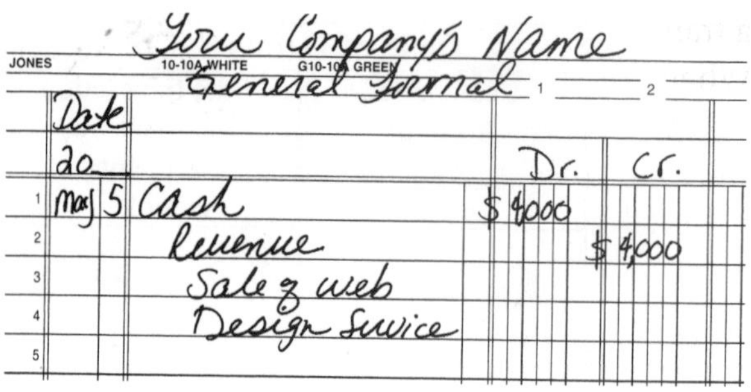

Figure 3.6

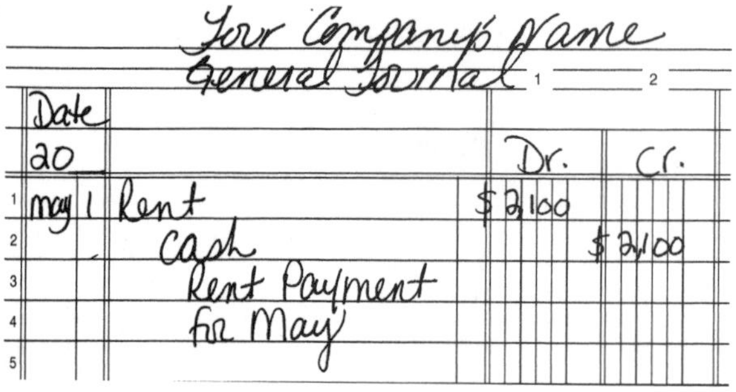

Figure 3.7

exception would occur in the case of an overpayment. When expenses are entered in the journal, the credit is usually to cash. (See Figure 3.7.)

SUMMARY

There are eight steps in the accounting cycle; the first step is recording a business's transactions in the general journal, or the book of original entry. This procedure is known as journalizing. The T-account was described as an expanded description of the double-entry system. You need to determine whether an item should be recorded as either a debit or as a credit. Remember, assets and expenses increase with debits; and liabilities, owner's equity, and revenue increase with credits.

A normal balance is the side—debit or credit—that causes the balance to increase. Sometimes a transaction affects more than two accounts. When that is the case, a compound entry is made. An important key to remember is that the total amount being debited must equal the total amount being credited.

EXERCISES

3.1 Using the worksheet in Figure 3.8, head up a journal for the Jones Company and journalize (enter) the following transactions:

Jan. 2	Owner put $10,000 in cash into business.
Jan. 3	Business paid rent expense of $1,000.
Jan. 5	Business purchased supplies for $50 cash.
Jan. 9	Inventory purchased for $900 on account.
Jan. 14	Sale of goods brought in $250 revenue.
Jan. 29	Owner took out $500 in cash.

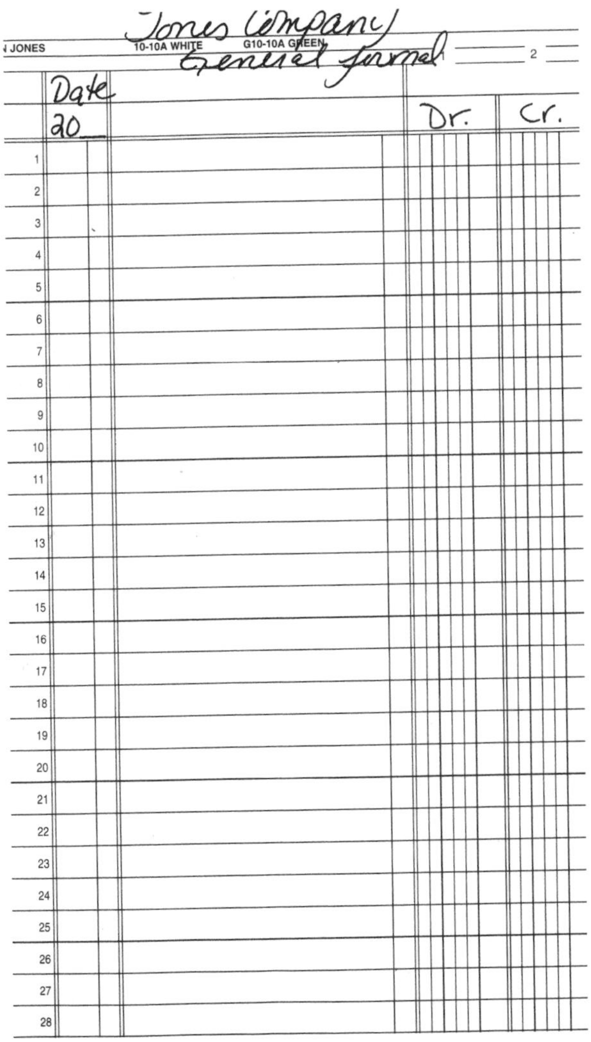

Figure 3.8

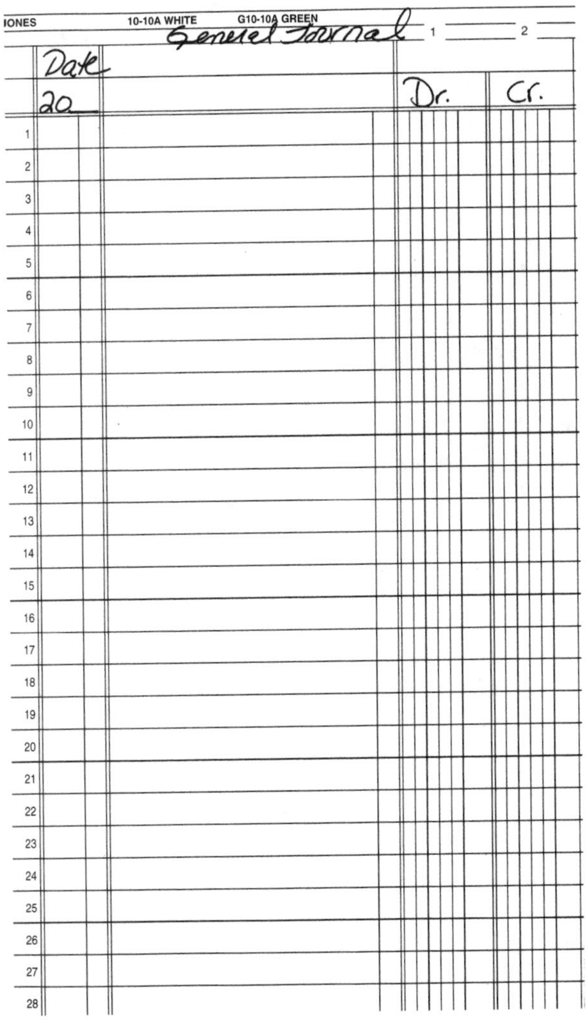

Figure 3.9

Skip a line between transactions.

- Remember to date every transaction.
- Begin by writing the year only, once on each page, in the upper left.
- Write the month below, once on each page. Do not write it again unless it changes.
- Then write the day for every transaction as shown in the preceding illustrations.
- The first entry will be a debit entry, followed by the credit entry, which is indented.
- Remember that every transaction must have a debit equal to the credit.
- Use the third line for a short explanation of what occurred.
- Put a dollar sign by first entry in debt and credit column.
- Indent credits.

3.2 Using the worksheet provided (Figure 3.9), enter the following expenses into the journal: rent $2,300, wages $2,000, telephone $120, website hosting fee $145, office supplies $250, and fire insurance $1,200. All were paid by check on February 12, 2006.

ANSWERS

3.1 See Figure 3.8A

3.2 See Figure 3.9A

Answers for **To Credit or To Debit** Sidebar

An increase in cash—Debit

A decrease in inventory—Credit

An increase in machinery—Debit

The spending of cash—Credit

Going into debt (increasing a liability)—Credit

Paying a bill that is due—Debit

Earning revenue from a sale—Credit

Increasing your (the owner's) equity—Credit

Jones Company
General Journal

Date 20			Dr.	Cr.
Jan.	2	Cash	$10,000	
		J. Young, Capital		$10,000
		Owner invests cash into business		
	3	Rent Expense	$1,000	
		Cash		$1,000
		Paid January 20__, Rent		
	5	Supplies	50	
		Cash		50
		Purchased Office Supplies		
	9	Inventory	900	
		Accounts Payable		900
		Purchased Inventory on account		
	14	Cash	250	
		Sales Revenue		250
		Sales for week of 1/14		
	29	Owner's Drawing Account	500	
		Cash		500
		Owner withdraws		

Figure 3.8A

General Journal

Date 20			Dr.	Cr.
Feb.	12	Rent Expense	$2300	
		Cash		$2300
		Paid Feb. 20__ Rent		
	12	Wages Expense	2000	
		Cash		2000
		Paid wages week of 2/12		
	12	Utilities Expense	120	
		Cash		120
		Paid phone bill		
	12	Advertising Expense	145	
		Cash		145
		Paid web site hosting fee for Feb.		
	12	Office Supplies Expense	250	
		Cash		250
		Purchased Office Supplies		
	12	Insurance Expense	1,200	
		Cash		1200
		Paid fire Insurance		

Figure 3.9A

CHAPTER 4

THE LEDGER

KEY TERMS

ledger, chart of accounts, cross-referencing, transposition error, slide error

When you enter transactions into the journal, they are in chronological order but otherwise mixed. Your next step is to transfer the transactions to a ledger. A *ledger* is a book of accounts in which each individual type of transaction is maintained separately. These accounts are used to prepare many kinds of financial reports.

For example, a ledger has a separate page for cash transactions so that the bookkeeper can know the status of cash at all times. A separate account is kept for each customer who owes the firm money and each vendor to whom the firm owes money. Once these accounts are established, the totals of accounts can be quickly determined. In addition, a separate ledger page is created for each asset account, for each type of liability, for owner's equity, for revenue, and for expenses.

KEEPING LEDGER ACCOUNTS

When transactions are recorded in the journal, we say we are "entering the transaction" or simply "entering." This term is even more appropriate today, since data is entered into computers. We will be discussing this in Chapter 18. First we must be thoroughly familiar with how all of these things work together. Transferring information from the journal to the appropriate page in the ledger is called posting. Since accounts in the ledger take the form of the letter "T," they are called *ledger T-accounts* (see Figure 4.1). Ledger T-accounts are similar to journal T-accounts in that the left column is called the *debit* (Dr.) side and the right column is called the *credit* (Cr.) side.

THE CHART OF ACCOUNTS

In their simplest form, ledger T-accounts may consist of sheets in manila folders. They may be pages in a binder divided by tabs. They are most likely kept on computer files.

Whatever form they take, each is assigned an account title and an account number. The title will be something like "Cash," "Payroll Account," or "Accounts Receivable, A Cut

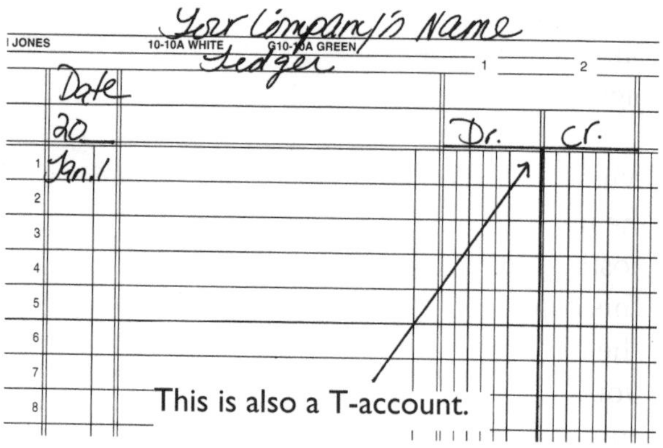

Figure 4.1

Chart of Accounts

Balance Sheet Accounts

1. Assets

10. Cash
11. Accounts Receivable
12. Supplies on Hand
13. Merchandise
14. Office Equipment
15. Prepaid Rent
16. Prepaid Insurance

2. Liabilities

21. Accounts Payable, Smith Co.
22. Salaries Payable
23. Taxes Payable
24. Interest Payable
25. Notes Payable

3. Owner's Equity

31. John Doe, Capital
32. John Doe, Drawing Account

Income Statement Accounts

4. Revenues

41. Sales Revenue
42. Service Revenue

5. Expenses

51. Supplies
52. Salaries
53. Rent
54. Insurance
55. Utilities
56. Web Hosting
57. Miscellaneous

Figure 4.2

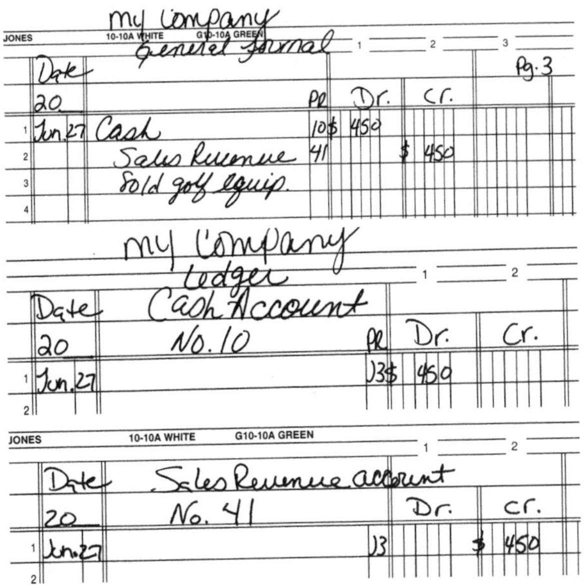

Figure 4.3

Above, Inc." A *chart of accounts* is a single index page that is kept to list all the account titles used in daily bookkeeping operations together with their numbers. (See Figure 4.2.)

Posting and Cross-Referencing

Each journal line must be separately carried forward, or posted, to its corresponding ledger account. Suppose you had a journal entry for June 27 as shown at the top of Figure 4.3. Your cash entry of $450 for the sale of golf equipment would be posted as a debit on your cash account ledger page and a credit on your sales revenue account, as shown in Figure 4.3.

When you have done this, you would enter the number of the relevant account in the posting reference column of your journal. This column is marked as PR in your journal. The number of your cash account is 10; this would appear beside the cash entry. The number of the sales revenue account is 41; this would appear beside the sales revenue entry. In the ledger, you would write J3 in the posting reference column of both accounts to indicate where the posted item came from. This system is called cross-referencing. *Cross-referencing* is the name given for the practice of using notes in journals and ledgers that show where the entries came from. Cross-referencing "leaves tracks" to facilitate an audit or locate a possible error.

Your posting must be absolutely precise because only perfect work will allow your books to balance. It is far easier to check your work as you perform it than to hunt for an error later on.

COMMON ERRORS IN POSTING

Several kinds of errors are common in bookkeeping; knowing what they are helps you locate them. For example, one of the most common errors is a transposition error. A *transposition error* occurs when you inadvertently reverse numbers when writing or entering them on a keyboard—for example, recording 67 instead of 76. All transposition errors create discrepancies that are multiples of 9. If you are out of balance and the difference between debits and credits is 9, or is evenly divisible by 9, look for a transposition error.

A *slide error* occurs when you unintentionally move a number over one decimal place, writing $10,000 instead of $1,000 or $100,000. Of course, it is also possible to make a slide error of pennies, but a discrepancy that is a large even number should alert you to look for a slide error.

You can also create errors by failing to post or by posting the same number twice. Again, take care when you are posting to avoid the tedious tracing of mistakes.

THE TRIAL BALANCE

At the end of the month (or other accounting period), when every item from the journal for that period has been posted to the ledger accounts, it is time to verify that the debits and the credits in the ledger are in balance. This procedure will determine the *trial balance.*

Your first step is to find the account balance of every ledger T-account. To do this, you must:

1. Sum (add up) the debit column.

2. Sum (add up) the credit column.

3. Subtract the smaller sum from the larger.

4. Write the remainder on the larger side.

Cash Account #10

	Dr.	Cr.
	$150.00	
		$75.00
	280.00	
	125.00	
		120.00
Balance	$360.00	

The account balance is determined by finding the difference between all of the debits and all of the credits for the account. This is accomplished by adding all of the debits to find their total value; you may record the answer on a separate sheet. Then total all of the credits for the account, similar to the debit side. Now find the difference by subtracting the smaller total from the larger total. The resulting answer is the account balance, which will be recorded on the side (debit or credit) that has the larger total. For example, if the total of all debits for an account equals $1,200 and the total of that account's credits equals $800, the account's balance would be a $400 debit ($1,200 – $800 = $400).

Is this a normal balance for the account? You can practice the account balance process in Exercise 4.3.

To continue with the process of making a trial balance, you need to calculate the account balance for each account in your ledger. The account balance is placed in its corresponding debit or credit column. You then make a schedule, listing each account's name, number, and balance. The sum of the debit balances should equal the sum of the credit balances. A sample trial balance is shown in Figure 4.4.

My Company
Trial Balance

Acct No.		Dr.	Cr.
10	Cash	$12,650	
11	Accounts Receivable	16,250	
12	Rent Receivable	1,500	
14	Inventory	32,300	
21	Accounts Payable, Jones		$1,850
22	Accounts Payable, Smith Co.		1,200
28	Notes Payable		6,500
30	Owner's Equity		5,310
40	Sales Revenue		72,000
52	Supplies Expense	960	
56	Rent Expense	3,500	
58	Utilities	1,200	
59	Salaries	18,500	
		$86,860	$86,860

Figure 4.4

WHAT TO DO IF YOUR TRIAL BALANCE DOESN'T BALANCE

If your trial balance doesn't balance, going through these steps in the suggested order ensures that you will find the error in the shortest possible time.

1. Find out the exact amount of your error: by how much are you out of balance?
2. Is the error $10, $100, or $1,000? You probably failed to carry when adding or to borrow when subtracting, or you may have made a slide error in posting.
3. Look at your debits and credits. Is there an entry exactly equal to your discrepancy?
4. Does the amount of error divide evenly by 2? Look for a duplicate debit or a duplicate credit posting where there should be one of each. A debit may have been posted as a credit or vice versa.
5. Does your out-of-balance number divide evenly by 9? Look for a transposition error. At this point, most errors have been located.
6. Add the trial balance columns again to check for accuracy. Next, recheck the addition while looking for a misread number. Sometimes a 1 is taken for a 7 or a carelessly written 3 or 5 may have fooled you.
7. Compare listing on the trial balance with each ledger account balance.
8. Recalculate each ledger account balance.
9. Trace each ledger posting back to its place in the journal. (Now you'll see the value of cross-referencing.) Check off each number in the ledger and in the journal as you verify it. Then look for numbers with no check mark.
10. Verify that journal debits equal the journal credits.

If, after all this, you have not found the error, consider changing occupations—or at least try to find the discrepancy again. There is no other place an error could occur!

PERFECT PRACTICE MAKES PERFECT

You have heard it said, "Practice makes perfect." This is not entirely true. A better saying would be, "Perfect practice makes perfect." If you are practicing but doing it incorrectly, then you will be very good at doing it incorrectly. This is another reason why we cover how to "do the books" on paper first. It is much easier to use a computer to help with bookkeeping if we know what we are doing without the computer. In typing or piano playing, practice builds both accuracy and speed. Bookkeeping is no different. The more often you perform these procedures, the faster and more accurate you will be. To give yourself the best possible chance of being accurate:

- Keep your workplace clean and uncluttered.
- Concentrate. Avoid noise and visual distractions.
- Carefully check and double-check with your mind and your eyes as you write each number and during each calculation.
- Avoid interruptions from telephone or visitors.

Some points to remember

- Transposition errors create discrepancies that are evenly divisible by 9.
- When discrepancies are large even numbers, they are likely to have been caused by slide errors.
- Locating an error takes far more time than being precise when posting.
- Being precise saves time and temper!
- An account is set up for each customer or vendor, each type of asset, each type of liability, and each revenue and expense. Entering information from the journal to ledger pages is called posting.
- At the end of each accounting period, a trial balance is prepared to verify that the accounts have been accurately posted.

SUMMARY

These are specific types of transactions that are grouped based on their effects on the business. A chart of accounts lists the title and account number of all accounts that the business will expect to use. Recording transactions from the general journal to the ledger accounts is called posting. Cross-referencing should be accomplished to aid the tracing of errors. Common errors in posting include transposition and slide errors. Follow the steps described earlier to rectify accounting errors if your trial balance does not balance. The trial balance is used to help ensure that posting has been done correctly.

EXERCISES

4.1 Practice posting the journal entries in Figure 4.5 to the ledger accounts on the worksheet (Figure 4.6). Be sure to enter each credit and each debit and to cross-reference every time.

4.2 Using the ledger accounts you created in Exercise 4.1, prepare a trial balance. You will begin by writing the name of each account in a vertical column on the left side of the page. Next, find the balance in each account. List these balances as debits or credits on Figure 4.7. Total the debit column and total the credit column. They should be equal.

My Company
General Journal

Date 20		PR	Dr.	Cr. Pg. 8
Ag. 4	Cash	10	2800	
	Sales Revenue	41		$ 2800
	Sales fr week 8/4			
7	Supplies on Hand	12	1550	
	Accounts Payable, Smith Co.	21		1550
	Purchased Supplies			
11	Cash	10	4100	
	Sales Revenue	41		4100
	Sales fr week 8/11			
14	Advertising	56	1250	
	Cash	10		1250
	Ad in newspaper			
18	Cash	10	3200	
	Sales Revenue	41		3200
	Sales fr week 8/18			
25	Cash	10	3850	
	Sales Revenue	41		3850
	Sales fr week 8/25			
29	Accounts Payable, Smith Co.	21	1550	
	Cash	10		1550
	Paid Supplier			
30	Wage Expense	52	2600	
	Cash	10		2600
	Paid wages			

Figure 4.5

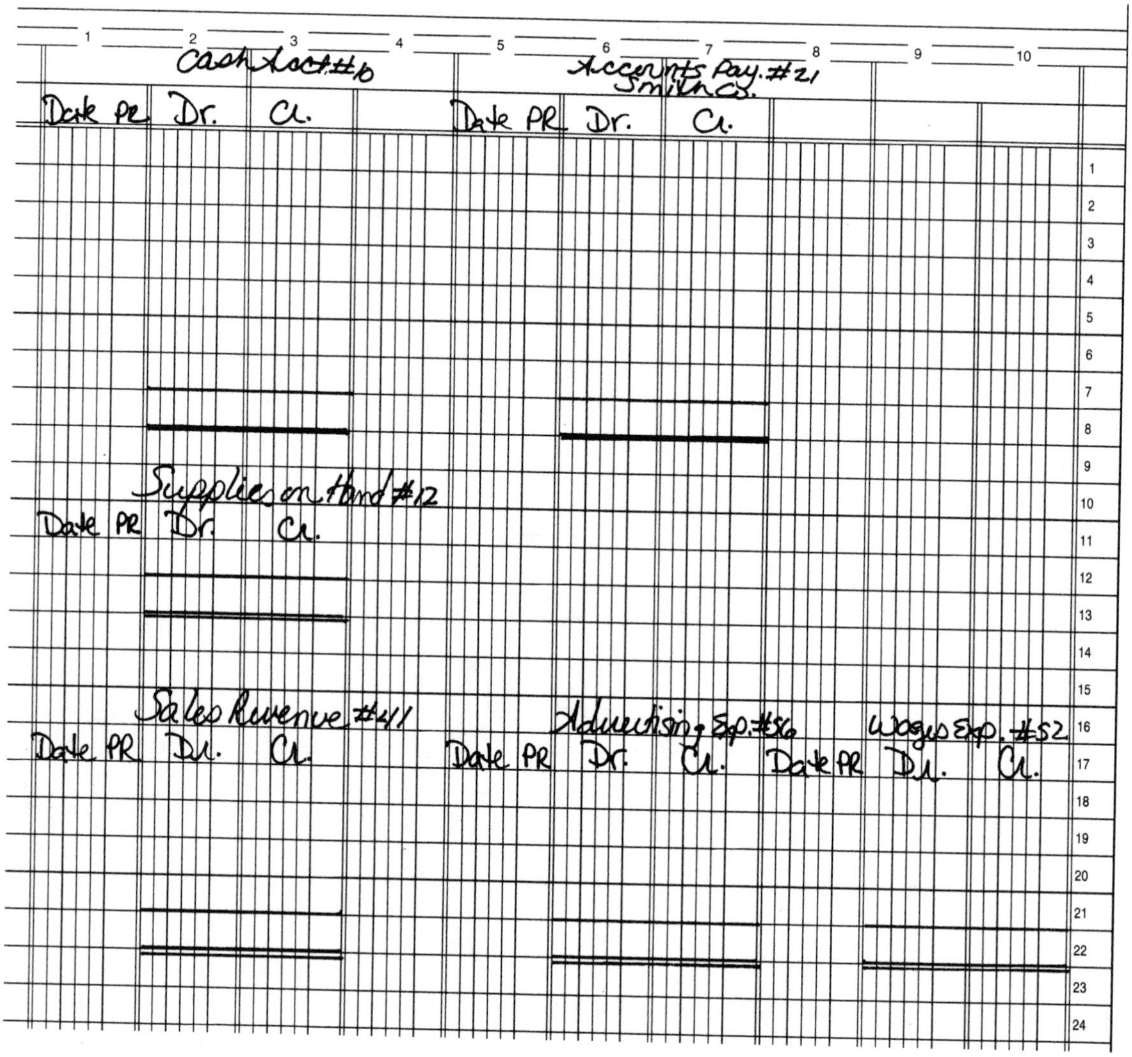

Figure 4.6

Trial Balance
August 30, 20__

Acct No.		Dr.	Cr.
10	Cash		
12	Supplies		
41	Sales Revenue		
21	Accounts Payable, Smith Co.		
56	Advertising Expense		
52	Wages Expense		

Figure 4.7

4.3 Find the account balance for the notes payable account below.

Notes Payable #21

Dr.	Cr.
-0-	$6,000
$2,000	-0-
$1,500	-0-
$1,000	-0-
-0-	$4,500

ANSWERS

4.1 See Figure 4.6A

4.2 See Figure 4.7A

4.3 See Figure 4.8A

Cash Acct. #10

Date	PR	Dr.	Cr.
Aug 4	J8	$2800	
11	J8	4100	
14	J8		$1250
18	J8	3200	
25	J8	3850	
29	J8		1550
30	J8		2600
		$8550	

Accounts Pay. #21 Smith Co.

Date	PR	Dr.	Cr.
Aug. 7			$1550
30		$1550	
			-0-

Supplies on Hand #12

Date	PR	Dr.	Cr.
Aug. 7		$1550	
		$1550	

Sales Revenue #41

Date	PR	Dr.	Cr.
Aug. 4	J8		$2800
11	J8		4100
18	J8		3200
25	J8		3850
			$13950

Advertising Exp. #56

Date	PR	Dr.	Cr.
Aug 14	J8	$1250	
		$1250	

Wages Exp. #52

Date	PR	Dr.	Cr.
Aug. 30	J8	$2600	
		$2600	

Figure 4.6A

Trial Balance
August 30, 20__

Acct No.		Dr.	Cr.
10	Cash	$8550	
12	Supplies	1550	
41	Sales Revenue		$13950
21	Accounts Payable, Smith Co.		-0-
56	Advertising Expense	1250	
52	Wages Expense	2600	
		$13950	$13950

Figure 4.7A

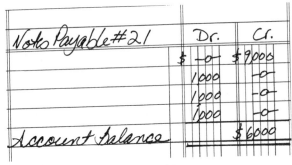

Notes Payable #21	Dr.	Cr.
	$ -0-	$9000
	1000	-0-
	1000	-0-
	1000	-0-
Account Balance		$6000

Figure 4.8A

CHAPTER 5

SPECIAL JOURNALS

KEY TERMS

special journals, purchase journal, sales journal, trade discount, credit terms, sundry account, controlling accounts

Every entry into a general journal requires at least three lines on the page: at least one debit, at least one credit, and a line for the explanation. If the business sold many items daily for cash or made frequent purchases of merchandise, the general journal would become crowded with entries and cumbersome to use. *Special journals* are used to group common types of entries into separate journals, simplifying the process of making manual journal entries. However, not every item on your chart of accounts will have its own special journal; only the active or busy accounts are selected. Special journals show both debits and credits on a single line and omit the explanation line. They are a condensed, single-purpose version of the general journal. It still remains true, though, that the total of debits will equal the total of credits.

Special journals are chosen according to the business's needs. Most businesses will use the following special journals: sales, service, cash receipts, cash disbursements, etc. Using special journals greatly eases the process of manually recording and posting transactions. Most premium computer programs designed for bookkeeping or accounting eliminate the need for special journals. They take the transactions from the general journal and post them to the appropriate accounts automatically. But not all businesses can afford to purchase these programs. Or perhaps they simply choose not to purchase them. It is important that we know how to use these special journals to increase our efficiency in manual bookkeeping. This knowledge will also make it that much easier for us to transition into a sophisticated bookkeeping program when that time arises.

TYPES OF SPECIAL JOURNALS

Many businesses receive cash often and pay out (disburse) cash in many transactions. Therefore, it is common to have both a cash receipts journal and a cash payments journal (sometimes called a disbursements journal). Figure 5.1 shows a typical cash payments journal. Compare it with the general journal shown in Figure 4.5 on page 29, and note the difference in the number of lines and style of entry.

In a firm where many items are purchased for inventory and eventually sold, it is common to find a purchase journal (Figure 5.2). *Purchase journals* are used to record purchases for inventory and other assets purchased on account (credit).

Similarly, a *sales journal* (Figure 5.3) is used if many sales are made "on account," that is, on credit. Note that two accounts are listed in one column.

JONES 10-10A WHITE G10-10A GREEN

Cash Payments Journal

Date 20		Ck. No.	Account Debited	1 Acct. Pay. Dr.	2 Sundry Acct. Dr.	3 Purch. Disc. Cr.	4 Cash Cr.
Feb.	1	101	Johnson Co.	$ 1,800			$ 1,800
	3	102	ABC, Inc.	2,800			2,800
	4	103	Phone Co.		$ 120		120
	4	104	Jones Equip.	1,500		$ 150	1,350
	5	105	Salaries	1,200			1,200
	8	106	Web Service		125		125
	9	107	Electricity		375		375
	10	108	Advertising	1,300			1,300
	31			$ 8,600	$ 620	$ 150	$ 9,070
				(21)	(X)	(#)	(10)

Figure 5.1

ONES 10-10A WHITE G10-10A GREEN

Purchase Journal

Date 20		Account Credited	1 Accts. Pay. Cr.	2 Purch. Dr.	3 Office Supplies Dr.	4 Store Supplies Dr.	5 Sundry Acct.	6 Amount Dr.
Mar.	5	Davis Brothers	$ 2,500	$ 2,500				
	6	Lincoln, Inc.	1,200	1,200				
	9	Buster's Place	9,400	9,400				
	10	Boone Distr.	820			$ 820		
	11	Medical Purchase	340				Office Equip.	$ 340
	13	Office Retail	1,245		$ 1,245			
	31		$ 15,505	$ 13,100	$ 1,245	$ 820		$ 340
			(21)	(51)	(54)	(56)		(X)

Figure 5.2

Entries in the purchase journal will be posted to a number of different accounts, such as accounts payable, office supplies, store supplies, and so on. The numbers in parentheses at the base of the columns (for example, 21, 51, 54, etc. in Figure 5.2) indicate the account numbers to which these entries are posted. The entries in the sales journal show the invoice number, the account debited, and the accounts (sales and accounts receivable) to which the entries will be posted.

Some examples of entries in special journals are shown in Figures 5.4 through 5.7. Figure 5.4 shows an entry in the cash receipts journal that records a transaction in which

Sales Journal

Date 20		Inv. No.	Account Debited	Accts. Rec. Dr. Sales Cr.
Jan.	1	101	Joe Cooper	$ 1290
	1	102	materials Inc.	920
	4	103	Harry's Yachts	560
	8	104	Sam's Accounting	1075
	12	105	Zimmerman, Inc.	1850
	31			$ 5695
				(10)(40)

Figure 5.3

Cash Receipts Journal

Date 20		Account Credited	Cash Dr.	Sales Cr.
Feb.	10	Farm Co.	$ 1200	$ 1200

Figure 5.4

merchandise was sold for $1,200 cash. This transaction results in a debit to cash and a credit to sales.

Figure 5.5 shows entries for a transaction in which the business paid a vendor (the James Co.) for an item that had previously been charged. This transaction is a debit to accounts payable and a credit to cash. (Payments made by check are recorded as cash payments.)

In the transaction recorded in Figure 5.6, the business purchased $4,850 in merchandise for resale from Gale Supply, Inc. This results in a debit to purchases and a credit to accounts payable.

When merchandise is sold on account, the transaction is recorded as a debit to accounts receivable and a credit to sales. Figure 5.7 shows that the Farm Co. purchased $6,875 worth of merchandise on credit. Note that the transaction is also debited to the customer's individual account.

DISCOUNTS AND CREDIT TERMS

As a bookkeeper, you will be dealing with several kinds of discounts or reductions from the list price of merchandise bought or sold. One of these discounts is a trade discount. A *trade discount* is a reduction from the list price of merchandise or a service that is offered to other businesses that purchase your firm's goods or services. Such discounts are commonly expressed as "20 percent (or some other percent) off list." If you made a cash sale of a $100 DVD player at 40 percent off list, you would record the sale as $60 in the sales journal, ignoring the discounted amount. If you sold a $500 air conditioner to an open account (a charge customer) at a 10 percent discount, you would record this transaction in the sales journal (and subsequently in the ledger accounts) at $450 ($500 less $50, which is 10 percent of $500).

Similarly, if your firm bought the air conditioner from a vendor (wholesale supplier) at 40 percent off the list price of $500, you would record this transaction at $300 ($500 less $200, which is 40 percent of $500). You would not record the trade discount.

Credit terms are the terms under which a firm sells to its open account (charge) customers. This is also known as the terms of sale. Often the terms are "net 30," meaning that the account is to be paid within 30 days of purchase. After that date, the account is past due, or delinquent.

N JONES G10-10A WHITE G10-10A GREEN

Cash Payments Journal

Date 20__	Ck. No.	Account Debited	Sundry Acct. Dr.	Accts. Pay. Dr.	Purch. Disc. Cr.	Cash Cr.
Jan. 1	101	James Co.		$1200		$1200

Figure 5.5

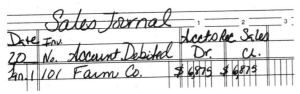

Purchase Journal

Date 20__	Account Credited	Accts. Pay. Cr.	Purchases Dr.
Jan. 2	Gale Supply, Inc.	$4850	$4850

Figure 5.6

Sales Journal

Date 20__	Inv. No.	Account Debited	Accts Rec. Dr.	Sales Cr.
Jan. 1	101	Farm Co.	$6875	$6875

Figure 5.7

To encourage prompt payment, many firms offer a discount—often 1 percent or 2 percent—to customers who pay within 10 days. These terms are often expressed as "2/10, n/30," meaning that the purchaser has 30 days to pay the bill but will receive a discount of 2 percent for paying within 10 days.

Suppose your firm, My Company, Inc., buys heating oil from That Heating Company on January 1 under terms of 2/10, n/30. The invoice (sales slip) total is $100, but the account will be considered paid in full if you remit $98 before January 11. Figure 5.8 shows how this transaction would be entered in your cash payments journal. The $2 that you deduct is called a purchases discount. The bookkeeper for That Heating Company would enter your payment in the cash receipt journal as shown in Figure 5.9. The discount you took would be shown as a sales discount.

To summarize:

- When the firm receives cash, *debit* cash.
- When a customer (outside account) pays a bill, *credit* accounts receivable.
- When a customer takes a discount for prompt payment (pays less than billed), *credit* accounts receivable for the amount

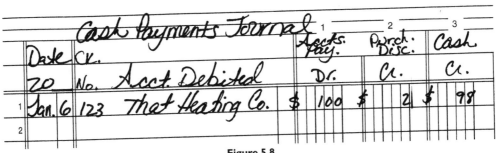

Cash Payments Journal

Date 20__	Ck. No.	Acct. Debited	Accts. Pay. Dr.	Purch. Disc. Cr.	Cash Cr.
Jan. 6	123	That Heating Co.	$100	$2	$98

Figure 5.8

Cash Receipts Journal

Date 20		Acct. Credited	Accts. Rec. Cr.	Sales Disc. Dr.	Cash Dr.
Jan.	6	My Company, Inc.	$ 100	$ 2	$ 78

Figure 5.9

Cash Receipts Journal

Date 20		Account Credited	Sundry Acct. Cr.	Sales Cr.	Accts. Rec. Cr.	Sales Disc. Cr.	Cash Dr.
Jan.	30	Interest Income	$ 385				$ 385
	31		$ 385 (X)				$ 385 (10)

Figure 5.10

of discount received *plus* the amount of discount legitimately taken; *debit* sales discounts for the discount amount; *debit* cash for only the amount actually received.

- Remember that "staying in balance" requires that each entry has an equality between debits and credits.

Turn to Exercise 5.1 to practice entering and posting credit sales and discounts.

THE SUNDRY ACCOUNT COLUMN

You have seen that special journals have columns reserved to represent the accounts commonly posted from a particular journal. Sometimes you will encounter a situation in which no column exists for a transaction. For example, your firm may not ordinarily receive cash payments of interest. You would enter such a payment in the sundry column (Figure 5.10). A *sundry account* is used to record infrequent or unusual transactions that have no column in the special journal. Transactions entered into a sundry column are subsequently posted line by line to the appropriate ledger accounts. The total of the sundry column is not posted.

Turn to Exercise 5.2 to practice using cash payments, purchase, and sales special journals.

SUBSIDIARY LEDGERS AND CONTROLLING ACCOUNTS

If your firm conducts business on credit, you must keep accounts to show how much money each customer owes the firm and how much the firm owes each creditor. Maintaining a large number of separate accounts within the main ledger becomes burdensome. Consequently, customer and vendor accounts may be kept in alphabetical order in separate folders, binders, or computer files called *subsidiary ledgers*. One subsidiary ledger would be the accounts receivable subsidiary ledger; the other would be your accounts payable subsidiary ledger.

Controlling accounts are kept in the general ledger and are one-page summaries of subsidiary accounts such as the accounts receivable summary account and the accounts payable summary account. It is important that the sums of the balances in the subsidiary ledgers agree with the controlling accounts.

SALES RETURNS AND SALES ALLOWANCES

Suppose a customer returns a dress to your employer's shop because it does not match the jacket she planned to wear with it. You would refund her the money, and the transaction would be called a *sales return*. Or perhaps a customer notices that a button is missing from a dress on display and she is given a price reduction. This is called a *sales allowance*. Both sales returns and sales allowances are reductions to sales revenue. If a cash refund is given, the sales returns and allowances account must be debited and the cash account must be credited. Remember that a credit to cash is reducing cash. If the item being returned was sold on credit, accounts receivable must be credited, and the customer's account must be credited in both the subsidiary ledger for accounts receivable and the control account.

A sales allowance may be handled like a discount. A credit sales return, however, generally requires that a credit memorandum be issued to document the amount that was credited to the customer's account. This may be a credit slip similar to a sales slip, or it may be a notice sent through the mail, or it could be recorded electronically. It reduces the total for that transaction from what the customer owes the business. The recipient may attach the credit memorandum to the new payment in place of a check for the amount due. This would not remove the customer's responsibility to pay another portion of the bill, if any.

HANDLING SALES TAX

Most states charge purchasers a sales tax stated as a percentage of the sale and require sellers to collect it. The seller's bookkeeper will credit sales tax payable, a liability account, for the amount of the tax.

For example, on a charge sale of $100 in a state with a 6 percent tax rate, the buyer would be billed for $106 ($100 plus $6 tax). When payment is made, the bookkeeper debits accounts receivable for the full amount of $106, credits sales for $100, and credits sales tax payable for $6. When the sales tax is paid to the state, the transaction is recorded as a debit to sales tax payable and a credit to cash. Computers have greatly simplified the accounting of sales taxes, but the principles regarding where debits and credits are entered remain the same.

SUMMARY

Special journals group common types of entries together using one line instead of the three lines normally required in the general journal. This greatly simplifies the bookkeeper's job, but does not eliminate the requirement that debits must equal credits. Different types of special journals include the cash payments journal, the sales journal, and the cash receipts journal.

Discounts are reductions in price, whereas credit terms are the conditions associated with borrowing money to purchase goods. Often a discount is offered for early payment or a penalty is assessed for late payment. Controlling accounts are one-page summaries of subsidiary ledgers.

EXERCISES

5.1 Using the worksheet provided (Figure 5.11), enter the following transactions. After you post the items to the worksheet, verify that the sum of all debits equals the sum of all credits. (Remember that, in actuality, you would post items for the entire month, or whatever accounting period you were using, before computing totals and balancing your accounts.)

Aug. 1: Received payment on account of $2,000 from R. Brown.

Aug. 1: Received payment on account of $490 from Blue & Sons in which a discount of 2 percent was taken from the $500 invoice.

Aug. 1: Received $1,600 from sales.

Aug. 2: Received payment on account of $900 from L. Hamit on which a 10 percent discount was taken from the $1,000 invoice.

Aug. 2: Received $750 cash service revenue.

Aug. 3: Received $90 from T. Gallagher in full payment of July bill.

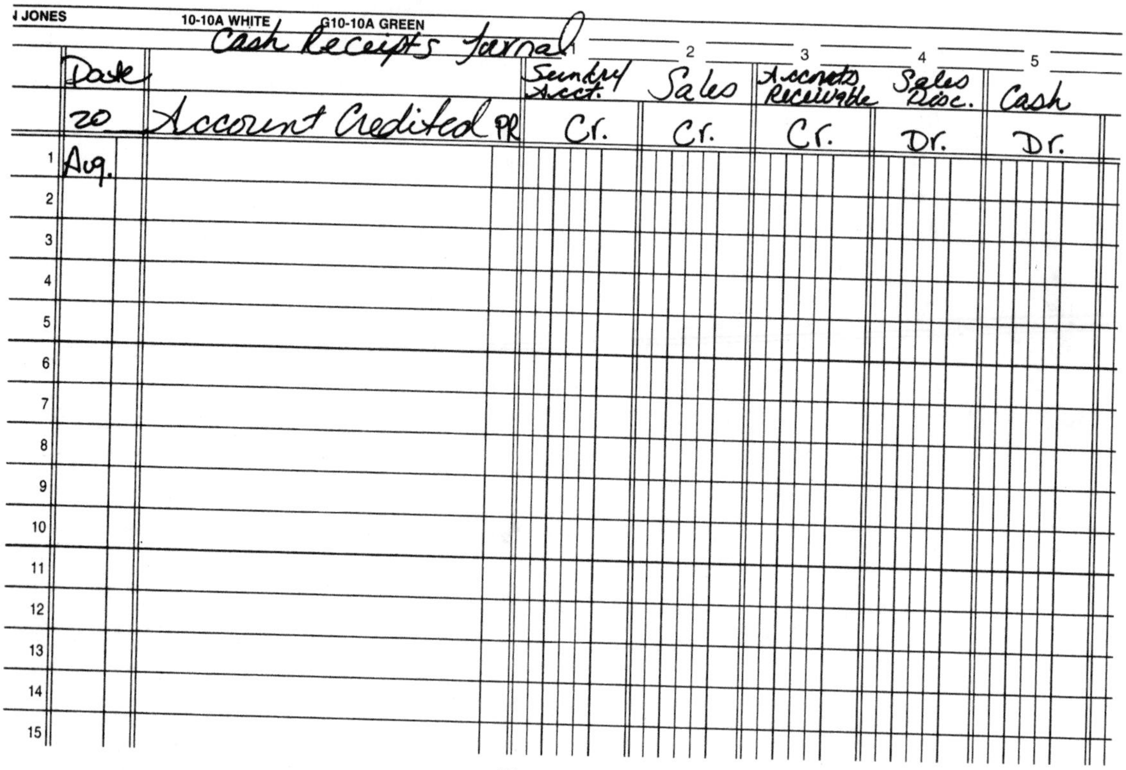

Figure 5.11

5.2 Use the worksheets (Figure 5.12) to enter the following transactions:

Sept. 1: You (your firm) purchased $1,200 in goods, paying by check (a cash purchase).

Sept. 1: You paid Volt Electric Company $980 after taking 2 percent off the purchase invoice of $1,000.

Sept. 2: You paid salaries of $800.

Sept. 2: You purchased $3,000 in merchandise on credit from A.V. Tronics.

Sept. 3: You sold merchandise on account to Ramco for $9,000.

Sept. 3: You paid Winston Brothers the $600 owed them, but took an allowed 10 percent discount and wrote the check for $540.

Sept. 4: Credit sales were $370.

Sept. 5: You purchased $200 in merchandise from Disk Company, paying $150 after discount.

Sept. 6: You paid advertising expenses of $95 by check.

Sept. 7: You sold the firm's old printer for $50 and sent an invoice.

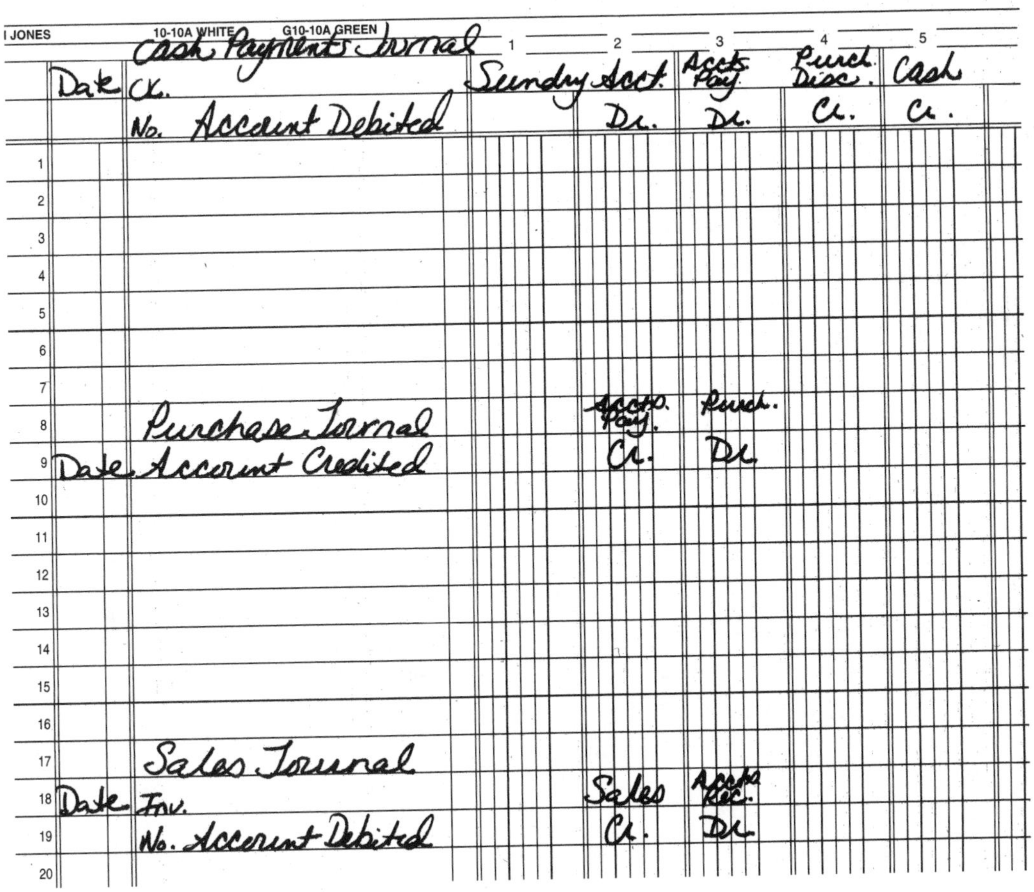

Figure 5.12

ANSWERS

5.1 See Figure 5.11A

5.2 See Figure 5.12A

NES 10-10A WHITE G10-10A GREEN

Cash Receipts Journal

Date 20		Account Credited	PR	Sundry Acct. Cr.	Sales Cr.	Accounts Receivable Cr.	Sales Disc. Dr.	Cash Dr.
Aug.	1	R. Brown				$2000		$2000
	1	Blue & Sons				500	$10	490
	1	Sales			$1,600			1600
	2	J. Flamit				1000	100	900
	2	Cash Service Revenue		$750				750
						90		90
				$750	$1600	$3590	$110	$5830
					$5940			$5,940

Figure 5.11A

Cash Payments Journal

Date 20		Ck. No.	Account Debited	Sundry Acct. Dr.	Accts. Pay. Dr.	Purch. Disc. Cr.	Cash Cr.
Sep.	1	1	Purchases	$1,200			$1,200
	1	2	Volt Electric Co.		$1000	$20	980
	2	3	Salaries Exp.	800			800
	3	4	Winston Bros.		600	60	540
	5	5	Purchases	200		50	150
	6	6	Advertising Exp.	95			95

Purchase Journal

Date		Account Credited	Accts. Pay. Cr.	Purch. Dr.
Sep.	2	A.V. Tronics	$3000	$3000

Sales Journal

Date		Inv. No.	Account Debited	Sales Cr.	Accts. Rec. Dr.
Sep	3	1	Ranaco		$9000
	4	2	Sales		370
	7	3	Office Equip.		50

Figure 5.12A

CHAPTER 6

THE WORKSHEET

KEY TERMS

unadjusted trial balance, adjusted trial balance, contra asset, adjustments to journal entries

You have now learned several of the procedural steps of a bookkeeper's job: (1) making a journal entry for each transaction, (2) posting journal entries to ledger accounts, and (3) making a trial balance. You also learned how special journals and subsidiary accounts fit into these procedures. These steps basically consist of gathering and recording data. Now you will begin preparing these figures to be used in financial statements that will be presented to the owners and managers of the business. This is very important because these reports will assist them in their financial planning.

USING THE WORKSHEET

Before you can make final financial reports for the accounting period, you will need to make changes or adjustments in your trial balance figures to allow for situations and events that were not recorded in the day-to-day entries and postings. For example, if you have not been making a change in your office supply ledger account each time a supply is used (which would be impractical in most cases), you will now have to take an inventory count of your office supplies to see the value of what you actually have on hand and adjust the account balance accordingly.

Furthermore, machinery and buildings wear out (depreciate) and an adjustment must be made to your capital asset accounts. (Depreciation is explained in Chapter 11.) You may owe wages, salaries, or commissions that have not yet appeared on these expense accounts because they have not yet been paid. The books may need to reflect that statistically a percentage of your customers will never pay their bills. It is one of those things that must be accepted in business.

The bookkeeper must take the initiative here because, unlike transactions, adjustments are not usually supported by paper documentation. You may have to request information from others in the firm, take inventories, or consult records from prior years to see what kinds of adjustments are generally required.

The worksheet simplifies making these adjustments and checking them for accuracy. It reduces the likelihood of errors in the final reports and simplifies preparing them. The worksheet itself is neither a formal report nor is it presented to anyone. Usually it is prepared in pencil.

Setting Up Your Worksheet

Generally, the worksheet has ten columns, which consist of a debit (Dr.) column and a credit (Cr.) column for each of five categories:

- Unadjusted trial balance
- Adjustments
- Adjusted trial balance

- Income statement
- Balance sheet

Some bookkeepers omit columns 7 and 8. We will discuss each of these categories in turn.

Columns 1 and 2: Unadjusted Trial Balance

You begin your worksheet by copying the trial balance data into columns 1 and 2 of the worksheet (Figure 6.1). At this point, some of the account balances shown will be incorrect, not because of errors but because adjustments must be made (usually at year's end) to update some figures. For this reason, columns 1 and 2 are labeled Unadjusted Trial Balance. Simply put, an unadjusted trial balance is the trial balance before adjustments are made to correct for unrecorded changes to various accounts during the financial period.

	Acct. No.	Account Name	1 Unadj. Trial Bal. Dr.	2 Unadj. Trial Bal. Cr.
1	10	Cash	$18,800	
2	11	Accounts Rec.	6,900	
3	12	Office Supplies	3,500	
4	13	Furniture & Equip.	34,300	
5	14	Accumulated Depr.		$8,200
6	21	Accounts Pay.		3,150
7	31	Capital Stock		15,000
8	38	Retained Earnings		8,300
9	40	Service Revenue		82,500
10	52	Salaries Expense	45,500	
11	53	Utilities Expense	1,650	
12	58	Rent Expense	6,500	
13			$117,150	$117,150
14	57			
15	59			
16	24			
17				

Figure 6.1

Columns 3 and 4: Adjustments to Trial Balance

Adjustments to the trial balances are first entered on the appropriate line in columns 3 and 4. Suppose you started the month (or other accounting period) with $3,500 worth of office supplies available for use. Now, at the end of the period, you have taken an inventory and found that only $1,300 worth of office supplies remains on the shelves. By subtracting $1,300 (the remaining amount) from $3,500 (the trial balance amount for the office supplies account), you find that $2,200 in supplies has been consumed in day-to-day use that was not recorded. You must adjust your trial balance to reflect this $2,200 change, which will eventually be shown on the income statement as an office supplies expense. An *adjusted trial balance* is a balance at the end of an accounting period (usually one year) that reflects changes not previously recorded in day-to-day accounting.

Figure 6.2 shows how these adjustments are made. The office supplies account has been credited in column 4 and debited in column 3. These paired adjustments are marked with a lowercase "a" in parentheses—(a)—so that they can be matched up when the worksheet is read. Later, you will identify other paired adjustments as (b), (c), and so on.

Now, suppose you learn that rent in the amount of $600 is due. It has not been journalized, since it has not yet been paid, but it will be an expense for the period in question. Figure 6.3 shows that a *debit* in column 3 has increased rent expense by $600 and is matched with a *credit* to accounts payable in column 4, line 6. These paired adjustments are labeled (b).

You now turn to the issue of depreciation. The depreciation calculated for furniture and

			1	2	3	4
	Acct. No.	Account Name	Unadj. Trial Bal. Dr.	Cr.	Adjustments Dr.	Cr.
1	10	Cash	$18,800			
2	11	Accounts Rec.	6,900			
3	12	Office Supplies	3,500			(a) $2,200
4	13	Furniture & Equip.	34,300			
5	14	Accumulated Depr.		$8,200		
6	21	Accounts Pay.		3,150		
7	31	Capital Stock		15,000		
8	38	Retained Earnings		8,300		
9	40	Service Revenue		82,500		
10	52	Salaries Expense	45,500			
11	53	Utilities Expense	1,650			
12	58	Rent Expense	6,500			
13			$117,150	$117,150		
14	57	Office Supplies Exp.			$2,200	(a)
15	59	Depreciation Expense				
16	24	Salaries Payable				
17						

Figure 6.2

fixtures for the period is $750. This is shown as a *debit* to depreciation expenses in column 3 and a *credit* to accumulated depreciation in column 4 (Figure 6.4). These entries are labeled (c).

Finally, you realize that, as of the last day of the accounting period, several days' pay will be due to the employees, amounting to $3,100. To reflect reality, a salaries expense must be shown as a *debit* and a liability called salaries payable must be *credited* with this amount. These adjustments are identified as (d) in Figure 6.5.

Columns 5 and 6: Adjusted Trial Balance

When you have entered all the necessary adjustments in columns 3 and 4, it is time to extend the totals to arrive at your adjusted trial balance in columns 5 and 6. If no adjustment was necessary for an account, then you simply bring the amounts from columns 1 and 2 over to columns 5 and 6. But if, for example, there is a credit in column 1 and a debit in column 4, you must *subtract* one from the other and enter the result, whether a debit or credit, in column 5 or 6, respectively. The answer will

	Acct. No.	Account Name	1 Unadj. Trial Bal. Dr.	2 Unadj. Trial Bal. Cr.	3 Adjustments Dr.	4 Adjustments Cr.
1	10	Cash	$18,800			
2	11	Accounts Rec.	6,900			
3	12	Office Supplies	3,500			(a) $2,200
4	13	Furniture & Equip.	34,300			
5	14	Accumulated Depr.		$8,200		
6	21	Accounts Pay.		3,150		(b) 600
7	31	Capital Stock		15,000		
8	38	Retained Earnings		8,300		
9	40	Service Revenue		82,500		
10	52	Salaries Expense	45,500			
11	53	Utilities Expense	1,650			
12	58	Rent Expense	6,500		600 (b)	
13			$117,150	$117,150		
14	57	Office Supplies Exp.			$2,200 (a)	
15	59	Depreciation Expense				
16	24	Salaries Payable				
17						

Figure 6.3

be recorded on the side (debit or credit) that was larger. Figure 6.6 shows how this is done for office supplies (account 12).

If column 2 and column 4 both show credits, they must be added, and the sum carried into column 6, as shown for accounts 14 and 21 of Figure 6.6. If there is a debit in column 1 and an adjustment debit in column 3, these are ***added*** and the sum put into column 5 (the adjusted debit column)—see the salaries expense line (account 52) of Figure 6.6.

To verify that you have performed these steps correctly, add up the columns. Columns 3 and 4 should be equal, and so should columns 5 and 6. If they are not, check your work on each line before proceeding. A simple way to remember whether to add or subtract is:

- When they are the same (both debits or both credits), you will add them.
- When they are different (one debit and one credit), you will subtract them.

Don't despair! The steps just described seem confusing, but with careful attention and practice they will become routine. Persevere at this point and you will gain a valuable

			1	2	3	4
	Acct. No.	Account Name	Unadj. Trial Bal. Dr.	Unadj. Trial Bal. Cr.	Adjustments Dr.	Adjustments Cr.
1	10	Cash	$18,800			
2	11	Accounts Rec.	6,900			
3	12	Office Supplies	3,500			(a) $2,200
4	13	Furniture & Equip.	34,300			
5	14	Accumulated Depr.		$8,200		(c) 750
6	21	Accounts Pay.		3,150		(b) 600
7	31	Capital Stock		15,000		
8	38	Retained Earnings		8,300		
9	40	Service Revenue		82,500		
10	52	Salaries Expense	45,500			
11	53	Utilities Expense	1,650			
12	58	Rent Expense	6,500		600	(b)
13			$117,150	$117,150		
14	57	Office Supplies Exp.			$2,200	(a)
15	59	Depreciation Expense			750	(c)
16	24	Salaries Payable				
17						

Figure 6.4

career skill. Don't allow yourself to be overwhelmed. Continue.

Columns 7 and 8: Income Statement Items

Now you are preparing information that you will use in calculating the income statement (Chapter 7). At this point it is useful to use a straightedge such as a ruler to guide your eyes along the lines. Focus on your adjusted trial balance columns (columns 5 and 6). Line by line, select *only revenue and expense items* and enter them in columns 7 and 8 according to whether they are debit or credit items.

Remember from Chapter 3 that revenue accounts such as sales revenue or service revenue normally carry credit balances. Depending on the nature of the business, these may include interest revenue, rental revenue, and so on. These are placed in column 8. Expense items normally have debit balances. Selected items such as salaries expense, utilities expense, supplies expense, and so on are placed as adjusted trial balances in column 7. These procedures are shown in Figure 6.7.

If you decide to add columns 7 and 8, do not expect the debits and credits to be equal. Inequality is normal here!

Acct. No.	Account Name	1 Unadj. Trial Bal. Dr.	2 Unadj. Trial Bal. Cr.	3 Adjustments Dr.	4 Adjustments Cr.
10	Cash	$18,800			
11	Accounts Rec.	6,900			
12	Office Supplies	3,500			(a) $2,200
13	Furniture & Equip.	34,300			
14	Accumulated Depr.		$8,200		(c) 750
21	Accounts Pay.		3,150		(b) 600
31	Capital Stock		15,000		
38	Retained Earnings		8,300		
40	Service Revenue		82,500		
52	Salaries Expense	45,500		3,100 (d)	
53	Utilities Expense	1,650			
58	Rent Expense	6,500		600 (b)	
		$117,150	$117,150		
57	Office Supplies Exp.			$2,200 (a)	
59	Depreciation Expense			750 (c)	
24	Salaries Payable				(d) 3,100
				$6,650	$6,650

Figure 6.5

Columns 9 and 10: Balance Sheet Items

Once you have transferred all revenue and expense items to columns 7 and 8, the remaining items will pertain to assets, liabilities, and owner's equity. Now you are entering information you will use in preparing the balance sheet for the period (see Chapter 7).

Assests will consist of cash, accounts receivable, supplies, furniture and fixtures, machinery, land and buildings, and any other property of value. The normal account balance for each of these is a *debit*, so they are put into column 9. A *contra asset* is an account that is charged against an asset. Accumulated depreciation is called a contra asset; because it is applied against capital assets; it is entered as a credit to column 10. Liability accounts, such as accounts payable or salaries payable, normally have credit balances and are entered in column 10. The results of these entries are shown in Figure 6.8. Take care not to omit any items that have been written on the bottom of the worksheet, such as salaries payable.

			1	2	3	4	5	6
	Acct. No.	Account Name	Unadj. Trial Bal. Dr.	Unadj. Trial Bal. Cr.	Adjustments Dr.	Adjustments Cr.	Adj. Trial Bal. Dr.	Adj. Trial Bal. Cr.
1	10	Cash	$18800				$18800	
2	11	Accounts Rec.	6900				6900	
3	12	Office Supplies	3500			(a) $2200	1300	
4	13	Furniture & Equip.	34300				34300	
5	14	Accumulated Depr.		$8200		(c) 750		$8950
6	21	Accounts Pay.		3150		(b) 600		3750
7	31	Capital Stock		15000				15000
8	38	Retained Earnings		8300				8300
9	40	Service Revenue		82500				82500
10	52	Salaries Expense	45500		3100		(d) 48600	
11	53	Utilities Expense	1650				1650	
12	58	Rent Expense	6500		600		(b) 7100	
13			$117150	$117150				
14	57	Office Supplies Exp.			$2200		(a) 2200	
15	59	Depreciation Expense			750		(c) 750	
16	24	Salaries Payable				(d) 3100		3100
17					$6650	$6650	$121600	$121600

Figure 6.6

Total columns 7, 8, 9, and 10. For columns 7 and 8, subtract the smaller total from the larger one and write in the difference below the smaller total.

- If the total for column 8 is larger than that for column 7, the business shows a profit in the amount of the difference.
- If column 7 totals more than column 8, the business shows a loss in the amount of the difference.
- If column 9 totals more than column 10, the owner's equity has increased during the accounting period by the amount of the difference.
- If column 10 totals more than column 9, the owner's equity has decreased during the accounting period by the amount of the difference.

Verifying Your Accuracy

The difference between columns 7 and 8 should be equal to the difference between columns 9 and 10. If the differences are not equal, then check your work. Notice that in Figure 6.8, the $22,200 at the bottom of column 7 equals the $22,200 near the bottom of column 10. The business has shown a net income, or profit, of $22,200 for this period, and the owner's equity has increased by that amount.

Acct. No.	Account Name	Unadj. Trial Bal. Dr.	Unadj. Trial Bal. Cr.	Adjustments Dr.	Adjustments Cr.	Adj. Trial Bal. Dr.	Adj. Trial Bal. Cr.	Income Statement Dr.	Income Statement Cr.
10	Cash	$18,800				$18,800			
11	Accounts Rec.	6,900				6,900			
12	Office Supplies	3,500		(a)	$2,200	1,300			
13	Furniture & Equip.	34,300				34,300			
14	Accumulated Depr.		$8,200	(c)	750		$8,950		
21	Accounts Pay.		3,150	(b)	600		3,750		
31	Capital Stock		15,000				15,000		
38	Retained Earnings		8,300				8,300		
40	Service Revenue		82,500				82,500		$82,500
52	Salaries Expense	45,500		3100	(d)	48,600		$48,600	
53	Utilities Expense	1,650				1650		1,650	
58	Rent Expense	6500		600	(b)	7100		7100	
		$117,150	$117,150						
57	Office Supplies Exp.			$2,200	(a)	2,200		2200	
59	Depreciation Expense			750	(c)	750		750	
24	Salaries Payable			(d)	3100		3100		
				$6,650	$6,650	$121,600	$121,600	$60,300	$82,500
	Net Income							$22,200	

Figure 6.7

Acct. No.	Account Name	Unadj. Trial Bal. Dr.	Unadj. Trial Bal. Cr.	Adjustments Dr.	Adjustments Cr.	Adj. Trial Bal. Dr.	Adj. Trial Bal. Cr.	Income Statement Dr.	Income Statement Cr.	Balance Sheet Dr.	Balance Sheet Cr.
10	Cash	$18800				$18800				$18800	
11	Accounts Rec.	6900				6900				6900	
12	Office Supplies	3500			(a)$ 2200	1300				1300	
13	Furniture & Equip.	34300				34300				34300	
14	Accumulated Depr.		$ 8200		(c) 750		$ 8950				$ 8950
21	Accounts Pay.		3150		(b) 600		3750				3750
31	Capital Stock		15000				15000				15000
38	Retained Earnings		8300				8300				8300
40	Service Revenue		82500				82500		$82500		
52	Salaries Expense	45500		3100		(d) 48600		$48600			
53	Utilities Expense	1650				1650		1650			
58	Rent Expense	6500		600		(b) 7100		7100			
		$117150	$117150								
57	Office Supplies Exp.			$ 2200		(a) 2200		2200			
59	Depreciation Expense			750		(c) 750		750			
24	Salaries Payable				(d) 3100		3100				3100
				$ 6650	$ 6650	$121600	$121600	$60300	$82500	$61300	$39100
	Net Income							$22200			$22200

Figure 6.8

JOURNALIZING THE ADJUSTMENT ENTRIES

To complete your worksheet, you will now need to enter each adjustment in the general journal. Remember, the journal is used to record all changes in the business. *Adjustment to journal entries* is the method of ensuring that all changes in the business are recorded in the journal. These are the items (a), (b), and so forth in columns 3 and 4 of Figure 6.8. For the entries made in this chapter, you would need to make the adjustments to journal entries that are seen in Figure 6.9.

In adjusting journal entries, follow the rules below. The terms "increase" and "decrease" refer to the normal balance of the account.

1. To adjust a prepaid item that has been consumed through the passage of time, increase the expense with a debit and decrease the asset with a credit.

   Example:
   Rent expense . . . . . Dr.
      Prepaid rent . . . . . . Cr.

2. To adjust a payable, increase the expense with a debit and increase the payable with a credit.

   Example:
   Salaries expense . . . . . Dr.
      Salaries payable . . . . Cr.

3. To show depreciation adjustment, increase the expense with a debit and increase the accumulated depreciation with a credit.

   Example:
   Depreciation expense . . . . . Dr.
      Accumulated depreciation . . . . . Cr.

Adjusting Entries	Dr.	Cr.
Supplies Expense	$2,200	
Supplies		$2,200
Rent Expense	600	
Accounts Payable		600
Depreciating Expense	750	
Accumulated Depreciation		750
Salaries Expense	3,100	
Salaries Payable		3,100

Figure 6.9

When you have completed the ten-column worksheet, you will be able to create an income statement and a balance sheet with ease, as you will see in Chapter 7.

SUMMARY

The worksheet is used to prepare data for use in financial reports. In Chapter 4, we learned about the trial balance. In determining the trial balance, not all of the accounts are recorded accurately. For example, the figure for office supplies is not really known until an inventory is completed. Thus, the trial balance is inaccurate until adjusted for these types of changes. The initial balance is therefore known as an unadjusted trial balance. After all adjustments have been made, a new trial balance is calculated. This is the adjusted trial balance. The adjusted trial balance will be used to generate two key financial statements. After the adjustments have been made, journal entries must be entered to document the changes. The work sheet is not a final report. Rather, it is a tool to ensure accuracy and completeness when the financial statements are compiled.

EXERCISES

6.1 Fill in the ten-column worksheet (Figure 6.11) for the Racket Company, using the information provided in Figure 6.10. After entering the trial balance in columns 1 and 2, record the following adjustments:

(a) Inventory of supplies on hand now shows $400.

(b) The prepaid rent has now been used.

(c) Depreciation for the month is $400.

(d) Salaries in the amount of $1,000 are now payable.

	Unadjusted Trial Balance	
	Dr.	Cr.
Cash	$3,000	
Accounts Receivable	2,000	
Office Supplies	2,400	
Prepaid Rent	1,200	
Tools & Equipment	1,000	
Accumulated Depreciation		$500
Accounts Payable		800
John Trout, Equity		6,500
John Trout, Drawing	3,000	
Sales		16,000
Salary Expense	11,000	
Miscellaneous Expenses	200	

Figure 6.10

6.2 Now use the General Journal sheet (Figure 6.12) to journalize the adjustments you have made in Exercise 6.1.

	Acct. No.	Account Name	1 Unadjust. Trial Bal. Dr.	2 Cr.	3 Adjustments Dr.	4 Cr.	5 Adj. Trial Bal. Dr.	6 Cr.	7 Income Statement Dr.	8 Cr.	9 Balance Sheet Dr.	10 Cr.	
1													1
2													2
3													3
4													4
5													5
6													6
7													7
8													8
9													9
10													10
11													11
12													12
13													13
14													14
15													15
16													16
17													17
18													18
19													19
20													20
21													21
22													22
23													23
24													24
25													25
26													26
27													27
28													28

Figure 6.11

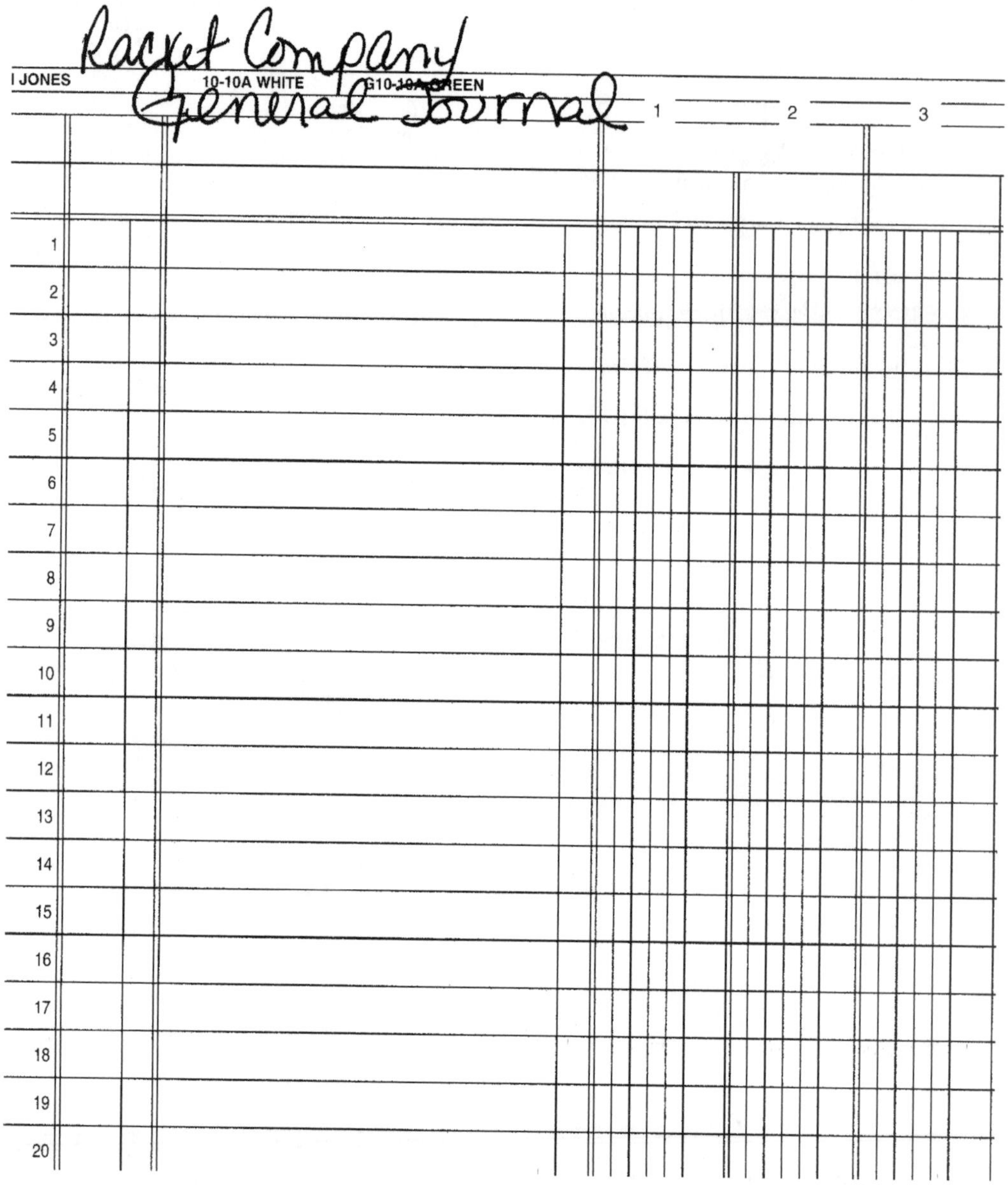
Racket Company
General Journal
I JONES
10-10A WHITE
G10-10A GREEN
1
2
3
1
2
3
4
5
6
7
8
9
10
11
12
13
14
15
16
17
18
19
20

Figure 6.12

ANSWERS

6.1 See Figure 6.11A.

6.2 See Figure 6.12A.

Racket Company
June 30, 20__

Acct. No.	Account Name	Unadjust. Trial Bal. Dr.	Unadjust. Trial Bal. Cr.	Adjustments Dr.	Adjustments Cr.	Adj. Trial Bal. Dr.	Adj. Trial Bal. Cr.	Income Statement Dr.	Income Statement Cr.	Balance Sheet Dr.	Balance Sheet Cr.
10	Cash	$ 3000				$ 3000				$ 3000	
11	Accounts Receivable	2000				2000				2000	
12	Office Supplies	2400			(a) $ 2000	400				400	
13	Prepaid Rent	1200			(b) 1200						
14	Tools & Equip.	1000				1000				1000	
15	Accumulated Depr.		$ 500		(c) 400		$ 900				$ 900
21	Accounts Payable		800				800				800
31	Owner's Equity		6500				6500				6500
32	Drawing	3000				3000				3000	
40	Sales		16000				16000		$16000		
51	Salary Expense	11000		$ 1000		(d) 12000		12000			
53	Misc. Expense	200				200		200			
		$23800	$23800								
55	Office Supplies Exp.			2000		(a) 2000					
58	Rent Expense			1200		(b) 1200					
59	Depr. Expense			400		(c) 400					
24	Salaries Payable				(d) 1000		1000				1000
				$4600	$4600	$25200	$25200	$15800	$16000	$9400	$9200
	Net Income							$ 200			$ 200

Figure 6.11A

Racket Company
General Journal

Pg. 9

	Date 20__		Adjusting Entries	Dr.	Cr.
1	Jun.	30	Office Supplies Exp.	$ 2000	
2			Office Supplies		$ 2000
3					
4		30	Rent Expense	1,200	
5			Prepaid Rent		1200
6					
7		30	Depreciation Exp.	400	
8			Accumulated Depr.		400
9					
10		30	Salaries Expense	1,000	
11			Salaries Payable		1000
12					

Figure 6.12A

CHAPTER 7

FINANCIAL STATEMENTS

KEY TERMS

income statement, net income, net loss, balance sheet

As soon as possible at the end of each accounting period, you should prepare financial statements. The most commonly used financial statements are the income statement, which shows income, expenses, and net income, and the balance sheet, which shows assets, liabilities, and owner's equity.

THE INCOME STATEMENT

A typical income statement is shown in Figure 7.1. An *income statement* is a financial report that uses a firm's revenues and expenses to indicate the financial performance of the business during a specific period of time, usually one year. Notice that income is classified by source and that sources vary from business to business. Sales revenue and service revenue are commonly included, but income from rent, interest, or other sources may also be shown. The source for the income statement is your worksheet; simply enter columns 7 and 8 from the worksheet into the appropriate layout as shown in the figure. Perhaps now you can see that even though the worksheet is an informal report, it is a very important tool. Expenses are listed below income. Customarily they are listed in declining order of value, although the owners of the business may prefer some other arrangement.

Net income, which appears on the bottom line, is often called "bottom line." It represents the earnings of the company (its profit). Sometimes net income represents earnings before federal corporate income taxes are computed (net profit before taxes) and another computation is made in which taxes are subtracted (net profit after taxes). For a proprietorship not subject to corporate income taxes, net income and profit will be the same. *Net loss* is the term used when total expenses exceed total revenue for a firm. Obviously a net loss is not something to celebrate, but it is not all that bad either. There are numerous reasons (beyond the scope of this chapter) that a business may incur a net loss. The ones to be concerned about are the *unintentional* net losses.

Sample Company
Income Statement
Year ended December 31, 20__

Income		
Sales Revenue	$ 146,000	
Service Revenue	218,000	
Total Revenue		$ 364,000
Less cost of Goods Sold		96,500
Gross Profit		$ 267,500
Expenses		
Wages and salary	92,300	
Rent	46,000	
Utilities	9,700	
Advertising	8,800	
Depreciation	8,500	
Insurance	7,400	
Office Supplies	6,200	
Licenses	5,100	
Repairs	3,200	
Bad Debts	2,400	
Miscellaneous	1,700	
Total Expenses		$ 191,300
Net Income		$ 76,200

Figure 7.1

In seasonal businesses especially, only the year-end accounting will truly convey the profitability of the business. Building contractors and farmers, for example, often show a loss in the first quarter of the year, and retail stores may count on making all or most of their profit in the final quarter.

Rules Regarding Format

Look back at Figure 7.1 again and pay particular attention to its format, especially indentations and the location of dollar signs and underlining. Bookkeepers differentiate between records kept in dollars and those using other measurements, such as weight or units sold. Someone unfamiliar with a particular document can tell at a glance whether it is a financial accounting, that is, dealing with money. Here are the rules for dollar signs:

- Place a $ at the top of each column representing money.
- Use a $ after every addition or subtraction, that is, next to every total or result representing money.

Similarly, there are conventions regarding underlining that convey information at a glance.

- A line is drawn beneath any column that is to be added or subtracted.
- Every final total sum is underscored twice.

Resist the temptation to be hasty. Don't underscore freehand. Instead, give your work a professional appearance by using a straightedge. Use a pencil with a very sharp point, not a dull point, and never a pen. Even the best bookkeepers are subject to occasional mistakes. Pencil lines can be erased neatly; ink cannot.

Regarding income statements produced by computer, be sure that the printer has plenty of toner and the paper is of good quality. Not only will the statement make a better impression, but also, photocopies distributed to management or to the bank will be easy to read. Remember, we will be talking more about the computer soon, but for now let's focus on learning the manual preparation of these reports. This will make our transition to computerized bookkeeping simple.

THE BALANCE SHEET

The income statement shows how much the firm has earned (or lost) during the accounting period. The *balance sheet* shows the cumulative effect of the firm's operations on the financial position of the owners. To create the balance sheet for your firm, you will use columns 9 and 10 of your work sheet. Figure 7.2 shows a typical balance sheet. Note that while the income statement follows the formula Revenue minus Expenses equals Net Income ($R - E = NI$), the balance sheet must balance.

Study the groupings in Figure 7.2. "Assets" (listed on the left) groups current assets and shows their total, then lists capital assets and shows their total. Note also that the amount of cumulative depreciation is shown on the balance sheet as a deduction from the original value of the equipment.

Liabilities (listed on the right) first lists the current liabilities, then long-term liabilities, then total liabilities. The owner's equity is arrived at with the formula Assets − Liabilities = Owner's Equity ($A - L = OE$) and entered beneath the total liabilities (which represents the creditors' equity).

Sample Jr. Co.
Balance Sheet
June 30, 20__

Assets			Liabilities		
Current Assets			Current liabilities		
Cash	$3,500		Salaries payable	$1,800	
Accounts Receivable	6,000		Accounts payable	2,100	
Office Supplies	1,400				
Total Current Assets		$10,900	Total Current Liabilities		$ 3,900
Assets			Owner's Equity		
Tools and Equipment	4,000		J. Trout, OE		10,200
Less Accumulated Depreciation	800	$ 3,200			
Total Capital Assets		$14,100	Total Liabilities & Owner's Equity		$14,100

Figure 7.2

DERIVING OWNER'S EQUITY

The original formula is A= L + OE. We can isolate owner's equity (OE) algebraically as follows: Subtract L from both sides of the equation to look like this, A − L = L + OE − L. When you complete that step, you will note that L − L will leave OE isolated on the right side of the equation, thus deriving A − L = OE.

Although you will initially create both the income statement and the balance sheet manually (unless you are using a computer program), most businesses require that the financial statements be finalized in typewritten form. The accounting manager or the controller, if the business is large enough to have one, will make a final check for accuracy before the typewritten statements are prepared or computer-generated reports are finalized.

Only one more step remains in the accounting cycle before it starts all over again. That step is to prepare the books for the upcoming accounting period. Closing the books is discussed in Chapter 8.

SUMMARY

The two most commonly used reports are the income statement and the balance sheet. The income statement comes from columns 7 and 8 on the worksheet. All accounts related to income are placed in the top section of the report. Expenses are listed below the income section. The total of all expenses is subtracted from the total of all revenue; the result is the net income. Net income may also be called profit or, in a case where expenses exceed revenues, would be known as a loss. The balance sheet shows the cumulative effect of the firm's operations on the financial position of the owners. The information used to create the balance sheet comes from columns 9 and 10 on the worksheet.

EXERCISE

7.1 Using the information on the worksheet for Exercise 6.1 (see the Answer section), prepare an income statement and a balance sheet for the Racket Company. Use the forms provided in Figures 7.3 and 7.4.

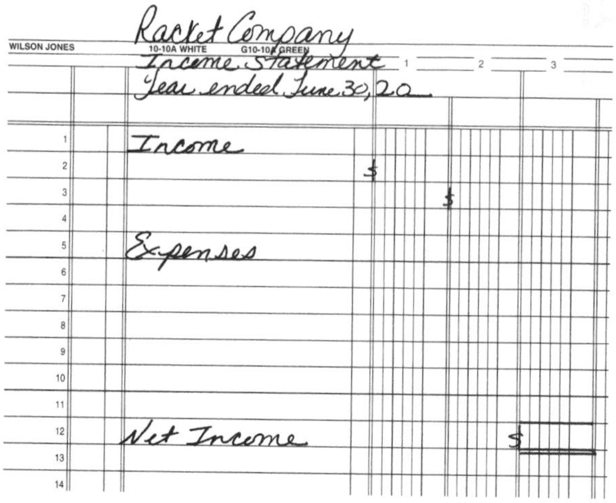

Figure 7.3

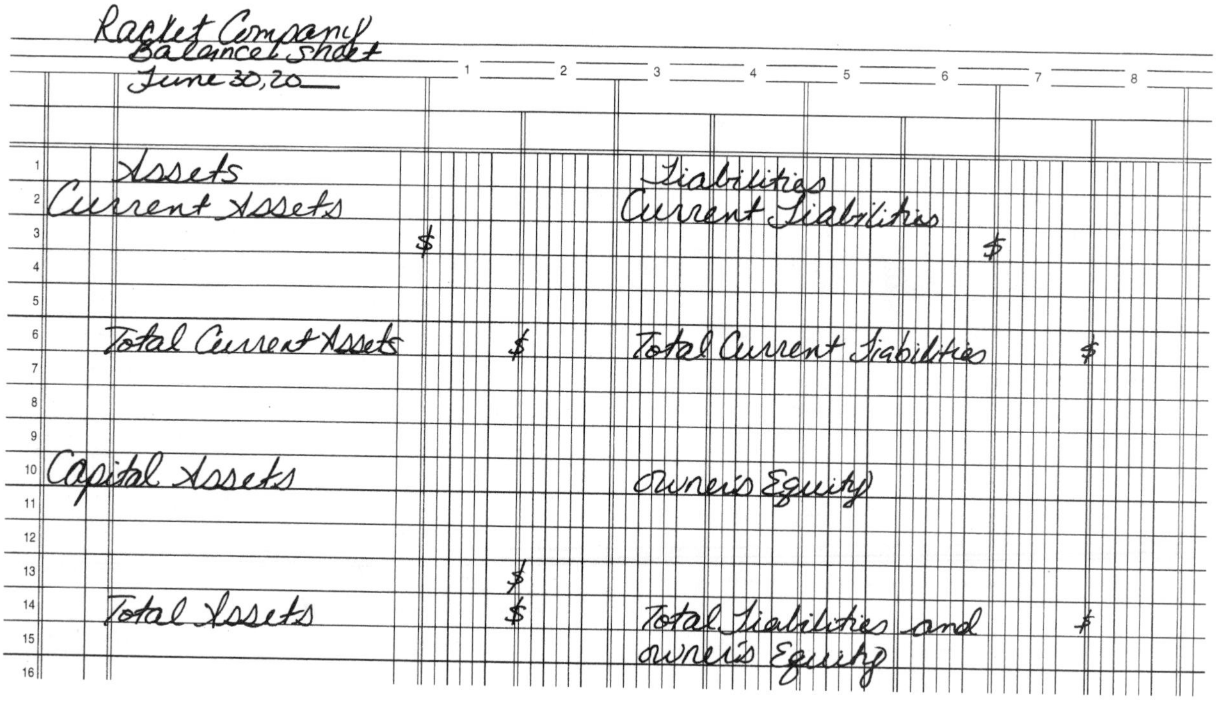

Figure 7.4

ANSWER

7.1 See Figures 7.3A and 7.4A

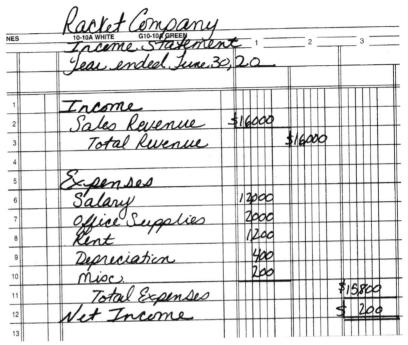

Racket Company
Income Statement
Year ended June 30, 20__

Income		
Sales Revenue	$16000	
Total Revenue		$16000
Expenses		
Salary	12000	
Office Supplies	2000	
Rent	1200	
Depreciation	400	
Misc.	200	
Total Expenses		$15800
Net Income		$ 200

Figure 7.3A

Racket Company
Balance Sheet
June 30, 20__

Assets			Liabilities		
Current Assets			Current Liabilities		
Cash	$3000		Salaries Payable	$1000	
Accounts Receivable	2000		Accounts Payable	800	
Office Supplies	400				
Total Current Assets		$5400	Total Current Liabilities		$1800
Capital Assets			Owner's Equity		3700
Tools and Equipment	1000				
Less Accumulated Depr.	900				
		$ 100			
Total Assets		$5500	Total Liabilities and Owner's Equity		$5500

Figure 7.4A

CHAPTER 8

CLOSING THE BOOKS

KEY TERMS

drawing account, income summary, post-closing trial balance

Your final task in the accounting cycle is to close the books. To *close the books* is to ready each revenue and expense account for the next accounting period, to adjust the owner's equity account by the amount of the profit or loss incurred in the previous period, and to reflect money drawn by the owner for personal use. The next few pages will lead you through the process. First, there are some new types of accounts to discuss.

THE DRAWING ACCOUNT

The *drawing account* is the ledger account in which you record money that the owner has withdrawn for his or her personal use. The ledger sheet is headed with the owner's name followed by the word "drawing." For example, "John Smith, drawing." For each sum drawn by the owner, you *credit* cash and *debit* the drawing account. When the accounts are closed, the debit balance in the drawing account is charged against owner's equity.

THE INCOME SUMMARY

You begin the process of closing after you have journalized every adjusting entry from columns 3 and 4 of your worksheet (see Chapter 6). A new T-account called *income summary* is an account created to summarize the information from all the revenue and expense accounts (and is only used when closing the books). The closing process consists of the steps listed in the next section.

STEPS FOR CLOSING THE BOOKS

The steps used to close the books are listed below. (See Figure 8.1.)

1. *Bringing revenue accounts to zero.* You *debit* each revenue account in the ledger in the amount of its balance, bringing the accounts to zero and readying them to receive the revenue of the next bookkeeping period. You then *credit* the income summary with the total of all revenues.
2. *Bringing expense accounts to zero.* You credit each expense account in the amount of its balance, bringing it to zero and readying it for the next bookkeeping period. You then *debit* the income summary by the total of all expenses.
3. *Balancing the income summary and adjusting the owner's equity account.* You find the balance in the income summary account (add the debits and the credits). If the firm has made a profit, you will have a credit balance. You *debit* the income summary by this amount and *credit* the owner's equity

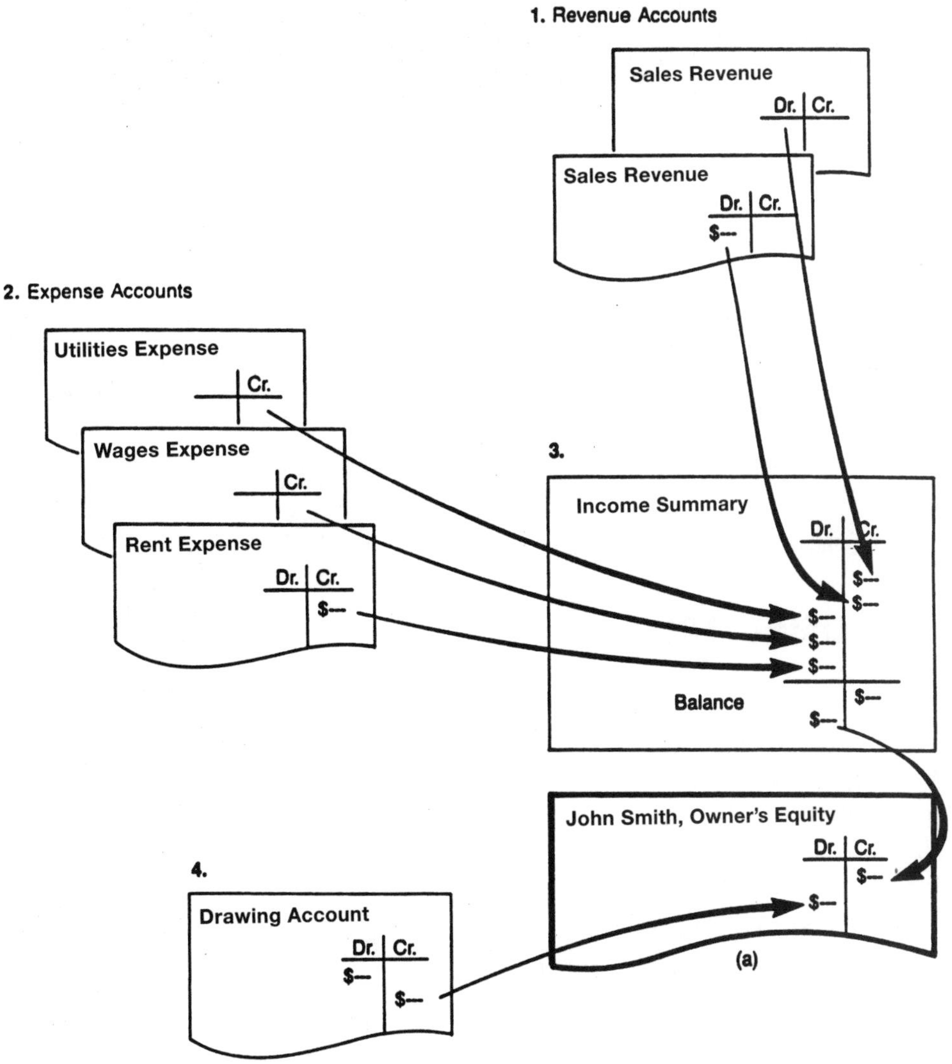

Figure 8.1—Closing the Books

account. A debit (minus) balance in the income summary account shows that the business has incurred a loss. You *credit* the income summary for that amount and *debit* the owner's equity account.

4. *Adjusting for the owner's "draw."* You *credit* the drawing account in the amount of its balance (total) and *debit* the owner's equity account in the same amount as previously described.

You would conclude the closing process by making journal entries for each step. The result would look like Figure 8.2.

The foregoing description assumes that the business is a proprietorship. In a corporation, you would have a dividends account (showing dividends paid to stockholders) in addition to the income summary. Both these accounts would be closed to the retained earnings account (see Chapter 17).

General Journal

20__		General Journal	Dr.	Cr.
		Closing Entries		
Dec.	31	Sales Revenue	$136,200	
		Service Revenue	97,300	
		Income Summary		$233,500
	31	Income Summary	128,700	
		Rent Expense		36,000
		Wages Expense		70,200
		Utilities		16,400
		Depreciation Expense		6,100
	31	Income Summary	104,800	
		D. Schmitt, Owner's Equity		104,800
	31	D. Schmitt, Owner's Equity	36,000	
		D. Schmitt, Drawing Account		36,000

Figure 8.2

THE POST-CLOSING TRIAL BALANCE

It is customary to take a *post-closing trial balance* to verify the accuracy of the closing process. After completing all the steps of closing, you list the balances in each ledger account (before they were brought to zero) in two columns, Dr. and Cr. The sum of the debits should equal the sum of the credits. At this point the accounting cycle is completed.

A WORD ABOUT CORRECTING ERRORS

Errors do occur; that is why a pencil is used in bookkeeping instead of permanent ink. However, erasures may raise questions about why the change was made. A better way is to draw a single-ruled line through an incorrect number and write the accurate amount directly above. This method clearly shows why a number was changed and promotes bookkeeping with integrity. We will discuss proper documentation and how to make corrections in computerized bookkeeping in Chapter 18.

SUMMARY

Closing the books occurs at the end of the accounting cycle. In the previous chapters we have moved from the original transaction all the way through to the financial reports for the period. Here we learned how to close the books to prepare them for the next period's transactions. This is important because, if the books are not closed properly, an inaccurate picture of the business's operations will result. Certain accounts must be brought to zero in preparation for the next period. These include all of the revenue and expense accounts that are zeroed to the income summary account. The income summary account is used for this purpose only. The owner's drawing account must also be zeroed. It is zeroed to the owner's equity account. The owner's equity account gets debited with a credit balance from the income summary account, indicating a profit. After making all of these adjustments, closing entries must be made in the general journal.

CHAPTER 9

TYPICAL BOOKKEEPING SCENARIO

This is a simplified look at what a bookkeeper may be expected to do. In this chapter, we will revisit the procedures covered in the previous chapters. Blank forms are provided so you can work along with the narrated text.

WALK THROUGH

You have just been hired to set up the books for Grimes Automotive Parts and Repair Shop. They have given you a stack of receipts and check stubs. The owner, B. Grimes, would like you to produce a chart of accounts, an income statement, "and all the other stuff you bookkeepers do, so I know how my business is going." The business was established on June 27 and opened to the public on August 1. We have all of the receipts from the establishment through October 31.

GETTING STARTED

Where do we start? First, let's put all of the receipts and check stubs in chronological order. This will make it easier to start journalizing the transactions. In Figure 9.1, you will find a completed general journal for all of the transactions. Later you will use the general journal to post the transactions to their respective ledger accounts.

SET UP A CHART OF ACCOUNTS

In order to set up a chart of accounts, we need to know what types of transactions the business will encounter. By looking at the general ledger, we can identify several accounts that need to be established, such as cash, supplies, inventory, etc. Since this example covers three months of operation, most of the accounts needed have already been identified. We should also inquire as to whether the business will require additional accounts, such as accounts receivable (if they will start selling on credit), depreciation expense, etc. It is better to have unused accounts than not to have enough accounts established to adequately portray the changes in the business. Use Figure 9.2 to set up the chart of accounts.

Figure 9.3 provides an example chart of accounts for this scenario. There will be differences between yours and the one provided in the book, and that is okay. The book includes a few accounts that have not been used yet but will be soon. Now that we have established a chart of accounts, we need to set up the ledgers so we can post the transactions.

POSTING THE TRANSACTIONS

We are now ready to label our ledgers in preparation for posting. We will be using Figures 9.4, 9.5, and 9.6 for the ledger accounts. You should notice that the account numbers have been provided to assist you.

Grimes Automotive Parts and Repair Shop

N JONES 10-10A WHITE G10-10A GREEN

General Journal

Pg 1

Date 20		Description	PR	1	2
June	27	Cash	10	150,000	
		B. Grimes, Owner's Eq.	30		$150,000
		owner invests			
		cash into business			
	30	Inventory	12	18,000	
		Cash	10		18,000
		ordered inventory			
	30	Equipment, Shop	15	10,500	
		Cash	10		10,500
		ordered diagnostic			
		machine			
Jul	1	Advertising	53	3,500	
		Cash	10		3,500
		Paid for ad and			
		signage			
	1	Misc.	58	750	
		Cash	10		750
		Paid for permits			
		and license			
	4	Advertising	53	550	
		Cash	10		550
		Advertising			
		materials given			
		away at town's			
		Independence Day			
		Celebration			

Figure 9.1

General Journal — Pg. 2

Date 20__			PR	Dr.	Cr.
Jul.	15	Prepaid Rent	16	2800	
		Rent Expense	52	1400	
		Cash	10		$ 4200
		Paid half month's rent			
		for end of July			
		and prepaid rent			
		for Aug.			
	20	Misc	58	2200	
		Cash	10		2200
		Paid for legal fees			
	23	Prepaid Insurance	17	1200	
		Cash	10		1200
		Prepaid 3 month			
		Ins. premium			
	28	Office Supplies	13	7500	
		Cash	10		7500
		Paid for office supplies			
Aug.	1	Rent Expense	52	2800	
		Prepaid Rent	16		2800
		expensed rent for			
		Aug.			
	8	Cash	10	5400	
		Sales Revenue	40		1900
		Service Revenue	41		3500
		Sales & Service Revenue			
		for week 8/8			

Figure 9.1 ***Continued***

N JONES 10-10A WHITE G10-10A GREEN

General Journal — Pg. 3

Date 20__			PR	Dr.	Cr.
Aug.	8	Wages Expense, Clerk's	55	$ 240	
		Wages Expense, Mechanics	56	1,200	
		Cash	10		$ 1,440
		Paid wages for week			
	8	Cost of Goods Sold	57	1,200	
		Inventory	12		1,200
		Record cost of goods sold			
	15	Cash	10	6,700	
		Sales Revenue	40		2,900
		Service Revenue	41		3,800
		Sales & Services Revenue for week 8/15			
	15	Wages Expense, Clerk's	55	350	
		Wages Expense, Mechanics	56	1,500	
		Cash	10		1,850
		Paid wages for week			
	15	Cost of Goods Sold	57	1600	
		Inventory	12		1600
		Record cost of goods sold			

Figure 9.1 *Continued*

General Journal — Pg. 4

Date 20__		PR	Dr.	Cr.
Aug. 22	Cash	10	$ 6750	
	Sales Revenue	40		$ 2650
	Service Revenue	41		4,100
	Sales & Service Revenue for week 8/22			
22	Wages Expense, Clerks'	55	430	
	Wages Expense, Mechanics'	56	1,700	
	Cash	10		2,130
	Paid wages for week			
22	Cost of Goods Sold	57	1,500	
	Inventory	12		1,500
	Record Cost of goods sold			
29	Cash	10	10,300	
	Sales Revenue	40		4,100
	Service Revenue	41		6,200
	Sales & Service Revenue for week 8/29			
29	Wages Expense Clerk's	55	400	
	Wages Expense, Mechanics'	56	2,500	
	Cash	10		2,900
	Paid wages for week			

Figure 9.1 *Continued*

N JONES 18-10A WHITE G10 10A GREEN

General Journal

Pg. 5

Date 20__		PR	Dr.	Cr.
Aug. 29	Cost of Goods Sold	57	$2,500	
	Inventory	12		$2500
	Record cost of goods sold			
30	Inventory	12	7,000	
	Cash	10		7000
	ordered inventory			
Sep. 1	Rent Expense	52	2800	
	Cash	10		2800
	Paid rent for Sept.			
1	Advertising	53	4,500	
	Cash	10		4,500
	Paid for Sept. advertising			
6	Cash	10	9,100	
	Sale Revenue	40		3800
	Service Revenue	41		5300
	Sale & Service Revenue for week 9/6			
6	Wages Expense, Clerk's	55	420	
	Wages Expense, Mechanics	56	2250	
	Cash	10		2,670
	Paid wages for week			

Figure 9.1 *Continued*

General Journal

Pg. 6

Date 20__			PR	Dr.	Cr.
Sep.	6	Cost of Goods Sold	57	2100	
		Inventory	12		2100
		Record Cost of goods			
		Sold			
	13	Cash	10	9000	
		Sales Revenue	40		3500
		Service Revenue	41		5500
		Sales & Service			
		Revenue for week			
		9/13			
	13	Wages Expense, Clerk's	55	380	
		Wages Expense, Mechanics	56	2300	
		Cash	10		2680
		Paid wages for week			
	13	Cost of Goods Sold	57	2100	
		Inventory	12		2100
		Record Cost of goods			
		Sold			
	15	Inventory	12	7050	
		Cash	10		7050
		Ordered inventory			
	20	Cash	10	12100	
		Sales Revenue	40		5600
		Service Revenue	41		6500
		Sales & Service Revenue			
		for week 9/20			

Figure 9.1 *Continued*

N JONES 10-10A WHITE G10-10A GREEN

General Journal — Pg. 7

Date 20__		PR	1 Dr.	2 Cr.
Sep. 20	Wages Expense, Clerk's	55	$450	
	Wages Expense, Mechanics'	56	2,700	
	Cash	10		$3,150
	Paid wages for week			
20	Cost of Goods Sold	57	2,800	
	Inventory	12		2,800
	Record cost of goods sold			
27	Cash	10	10,800	
	Sales Revenue	40		4,800
	Service Revenue	41		6,000
	Sales & Service Revenue for week 9/27			
27	Wages Expense, Clerk's	55	490	
	Wages Expense, Mechanics'	56	2,400	
	Cash	10		2,890
	Paid wages for week			
27	Cost of Goods Sold	57	2,500	
	Inventory	12		2,500
	Record cost of goods sold			
28	B. Grimes, Drawing	31	1,500	
	Cash	10		1,500
	owner withdrawal for personal use			

Figure 9.1 *Continued*

General Journal

1 2 3

Pg. 8

Date 20__			PR	Dr.	Cr.
Oct.	1	Rent Expense	525	$ 2800	
		Cash	10		$ 2800
		Paid rent for Oct.			
	1	Advertising Expense	53	2100	
		Cash	10		2100
		Paid for Oct.			
		Advertising			
	4	Cash	10	10550	
		Sales Revenue	40		4300
		Service Revenue	41		6250
		Sales & Service			
		Revenue for week			
		10/4			
	4	Wages Expense, Clerk's	55	480	
		Wages Expense, Mechanics	56	2550	
		Cash	10		3030
		paid wages for the			
		week			
	4	Cost of Goods Sold	57	2200	
		Inventory	12		2200
		Record cost of goods			
		sold			

Figure 9.1 *Continued*

N JONES 10-10A WHITE G10-10A GREEN

General Journal

1 2 3

Pg. 9

Date		Description	PR	Dr.	Cr.
20					
Oct.	11	Cash	10	$106 00	
		Sales Revenue	40		$45 00
		Service Revenue	41		61 00
		Sales & Service			
		Revenue for week			
		10/11			
	11	Wages Expense, Clerk's	55	5 00	
		Wages Expense, Mechanics	56	24 50	
		Cash	10		29 50
		paid wages for week			
	11	Cost of Goods Sold	57	24 50	
		Inventory	12		24 50
		Record Cost of goods			
		sold			
	15	Misc.	58	3 95	
		Cash	10		3 95
		ordered magazine			
		subscriptions			
	18	Cash	10	83 00	
		Sales Revenue	40		31 00
		Service Revenue	41		52 00
		Sales & Service			
		revenue for week			
		10/18			

Figure 9.1 *Continued*

N JONES 10-10A WHITE G10-10A GREEN

General Journal

Pg. 10

Date 20__		Description	PR	Dr.	Cr.
Oct.	18	Wages Expense, Clerk's	55	$ 475	
		Wages Expense, Mechanics	56	2,100	
		Cash	10		$ 2,575
		Paid wages for week			
	18	Cost of Goods Sold	57	1,800	
		Inventory	12		1,800
		Record cost of goods sold			
	25	Cash	10	10,800	
		Sales Revenue	40		4,800
		Service Revenue	41		6,000
		Sales & Service Revenue for week 10/25			
	25	Wages Expense, Clerk's	55	490	
		Wages Expense, Mechanics	56	2,400	
		Cash	10		2,890
		paid wages for week			
	25	Cost of Goods Sold	57	2,500	
		Inventory	12		2,500
		Record cost of goods sold			
	28	B. Grimes, Drawing	31	10,500	
		Cash	10		10,500
		owner withdrawal for personal use			

Figure 9.1 ***Continued***

After you have successfully labeled the ledger accounts, you must begin to post the transactions. Take your time; see Chapter 4 if you need help.

Now that you have posted the entries, it is time to obtain a trial balance.

Chart of Accounts

Assets
10
11
12
13
14
15
16
17

Liabilities
20
21

Owner's Equity
30
31

Revenues
40
41

Expenses
51
52
53
54
55
56
57
58

Figure 9.2

Chart of Accounts

Assets

10	Cash
11	Accounts Receivable
12	Inventory
13	Supplies (Office)
14	Office Equipment
15	Equipment Shop
16	Prepaid Rent
17	PPD Insurance

Liabilities

20	Accounts Payable
21	Sundries Payable

Owner's Equity

30	Owner's Equity, B. Grimes
31	Drawing, B. Grimes

Revenues

40	Sales Revenue
41	Service Revenue

Expenses

51	Supplies
52	Rent
53	Advertising
54	Insurance
55	Wages Expense—Clerical
56	Wages Expense—Mechanical
57	Cost of Goods Sold
58	Misc.

Figure 9.3

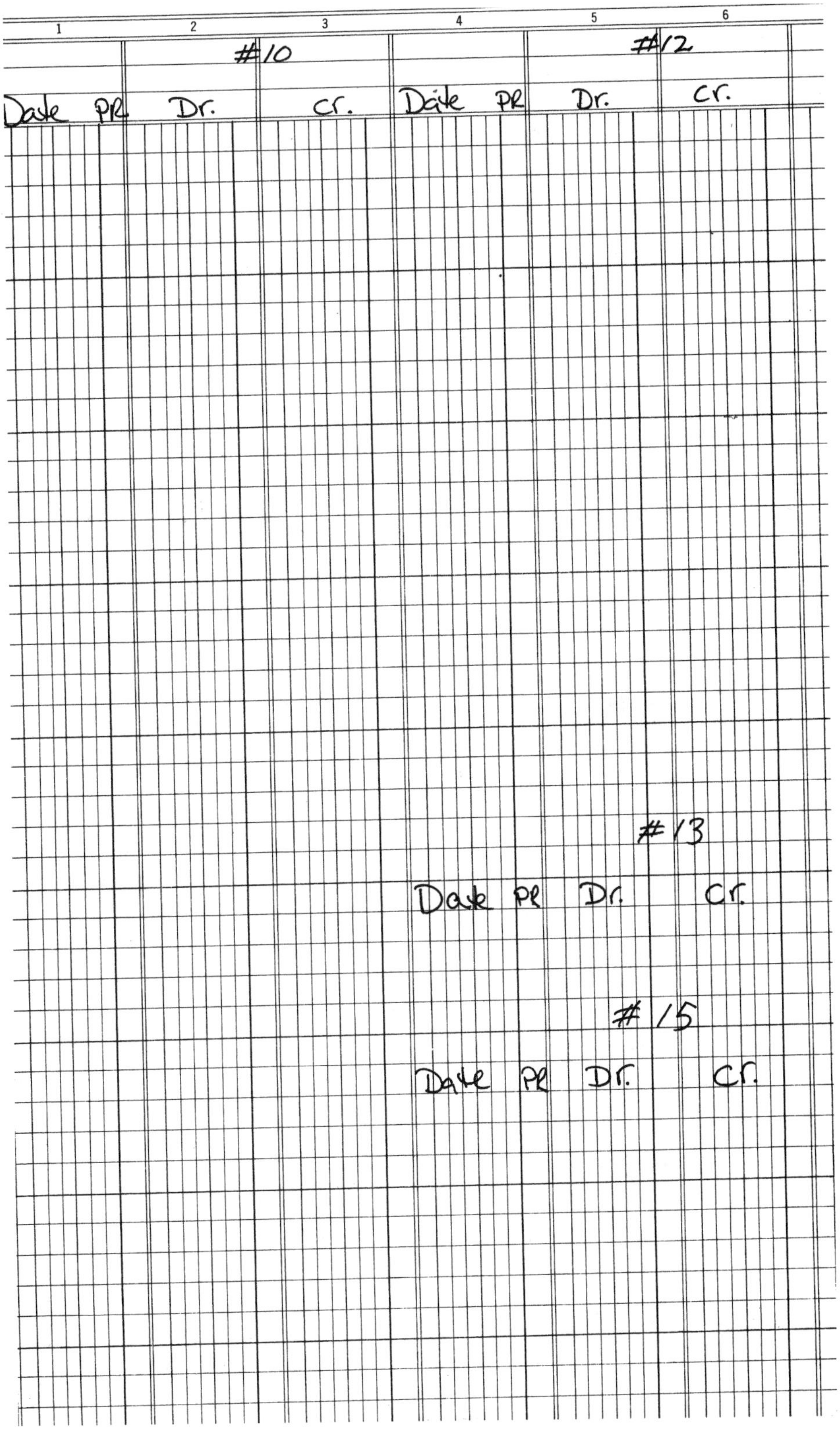
1 2 3 4 5 6
#10
#12
Date PR Dr. Cr. Date PR Dr. Cr.
#13
Date PR Dr. Cr.
#15
Date PR Dr. Cr.

Figure 9.4

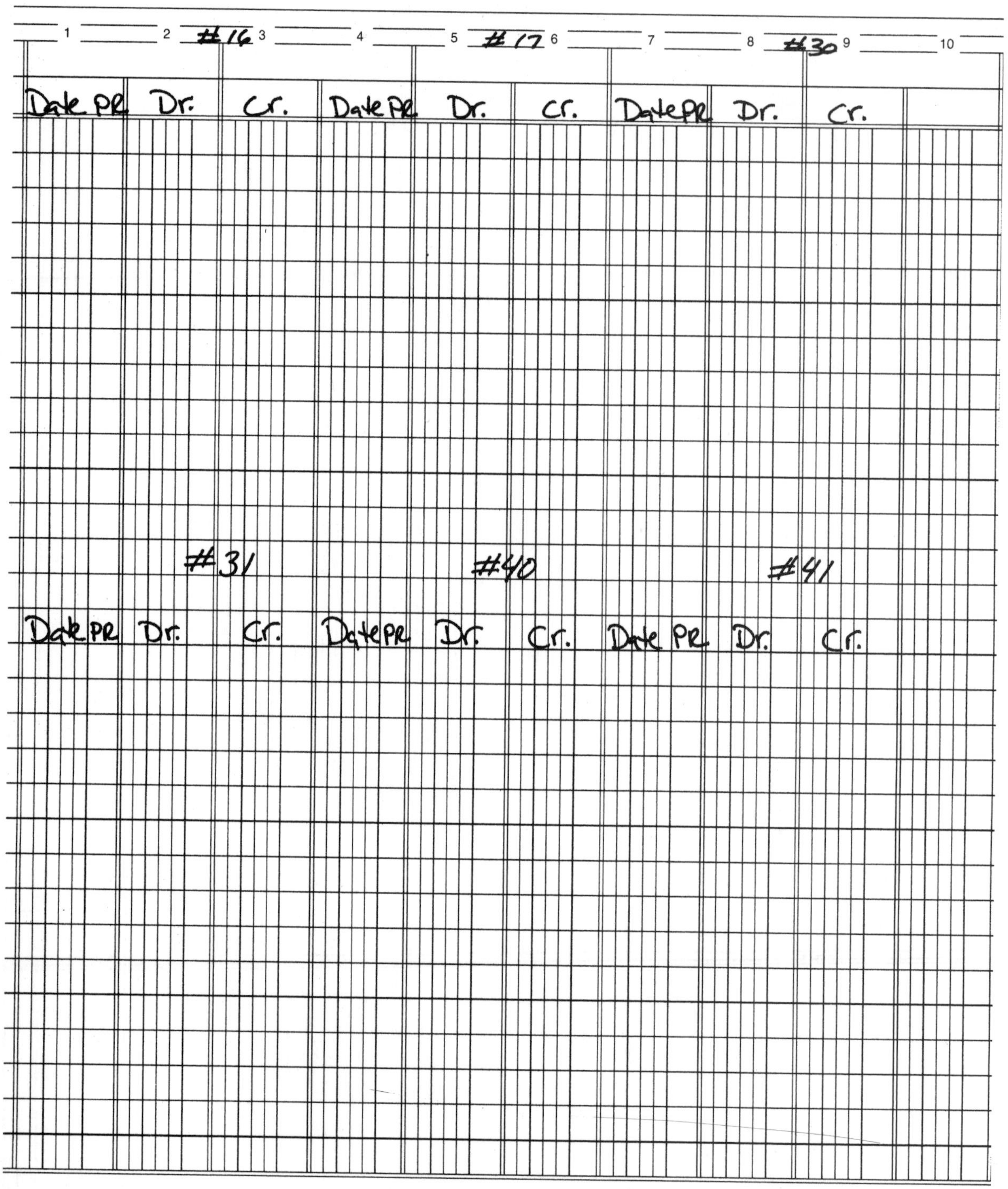
1 2 #16 3 4 5 #17 6 7 8 #30 9 10
Date PR Dr. Cr. Date PR Dr. Cr. Date PR Dr. Cr.
#31 #40 #41
Date PR Dr. Cr. Date PR Dr. Cr. Date PR Dr. Cr.

Figure 9.5

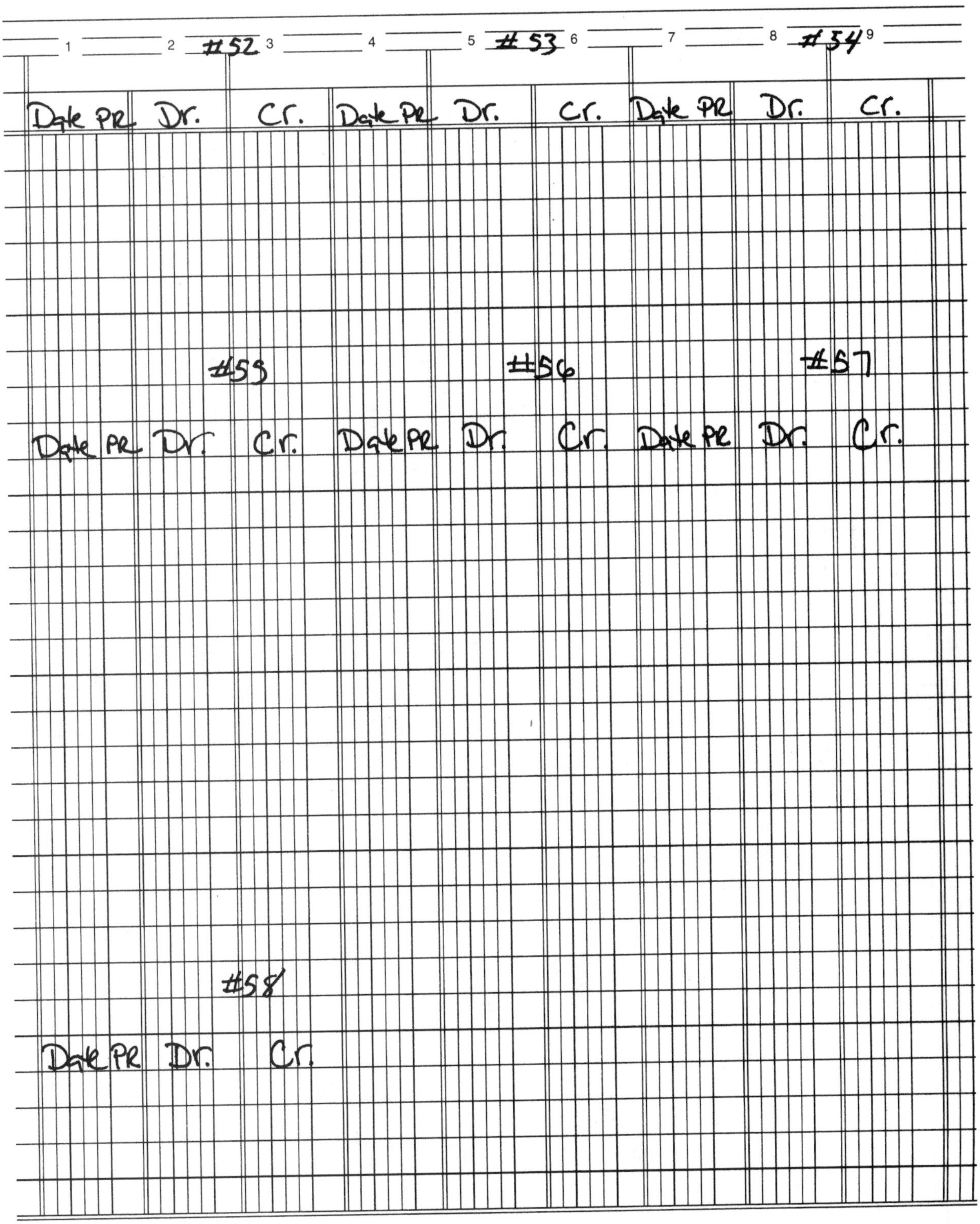
1
2
#52
3
4
5
#53
6
7
8
#54
9
Date PR Dr. Cr.
Date PR Dr. Cr.
Date PR Dr. Cr.
#55
#56
#57
Date PR Dr. Cr.
Date PR Dr. Cr.
Date PR Dr. Cr.
#58
Date PR Dr. Cr.

Figure 9.6

I JONES 10-10A WHITE G10-10A GREEN

Grimes Automotive Parts and Repair Shop

October 31, 20__

	Acct. No.	Account Name	1 Unadj. Trial Bal. Dr.	2 Unadj. Trial Bal. Cr.	3 Adjustments Dr.	4 Adjustments Cr.	5 Adj. Trial Bal. Dr.	6 Adj. Trial Bal. Cr.	7 Income Statement Dr.	8 Income Statement Cr.	9 Balance Sheet Dr.	10 Balance Sheet Cr.	
1	10	Cash											1
2	12	Inventory											2
3	13	Office Supplies											3
4	15	Tools & Equipment											4
5	16	Prepaid Rent											5
6	17	Prepaid Insurance											6
7	20	Accounts Payable											7
8	21	Salaries Payable											8
9	30	Owners Equity											9
10	31	B. Grimes, Drawing											10
11	40	Sales Revenue											11
12	41	Service Revenue											12
13	51	Office Supplies Exp.											13
14	52	Rent Expense											14
15	53	Advertising Expense											15
16	54	Insurance Expense											16
17	55	Wages, Clerk											17
18	56	Wages, Mechanic											18
19	57	Cost of Goods Sold											19
20	58	Misc.											20
21		Total											21
22		Net Income											22
23													23
24													24

Figure 9.7

PREPARING THE WORKSHEET

Obtaining a Trial Balance

The first step is to get a balance from each ledger T-account. Record the balances in the appropriate columns on the worksheet, Figure 9.7. Add all the debits and record the answer above the double-underscored space in the debit column. Do the same for the credits. Do they equal each other? If not refer to Chapter 4, page 25.

Adjustments to the Trial Balance

The following adjustments need to be made to the trial balance. There are $5,200 worth of office supplies remaining. An inventory of merchandise for sale indicates $120 lost. A refund of $85 was received from the state licensure board (business was inadvertently overcharged).

Let's look at these items, one at a time. The business has $5,200 in office supplies remaining. How much did it use during this period? Well, it started with $7,500, so $7,500 minus $5,200 equals $2,300. Therefore, the business used $2,300 worth of office supplies in this period. We need to adjust the office supplies account by $2,300. Which column do we use to record the adjustment? Remember, the office supplies account is an asset account. The normal balance for an asset account is a debit (Chapter 3). If you want to reduce an account that has a normal balance of a debit, you will credit that account. Remember, in order to keep the equation balanced, we are going to have to debit something. What will we debit? The answer is supplies expense.

The inventory shows that $120 was lost, probably through theft. Again, an asset account is being reduced, so we will *credit* the inventory account by $120 and *debit* the cost of goods sold by $120. The refund will cause us to *debit* cash and *credit* the sundry account, since this is where we recorded the licensing expense. Earlier we recorded $400 for insurance expense but should have recorded a total of $1,200 ($800 more than was recorded). This means we have an $800 adjustment to be made. We will debit insurance expense and credit prepaid insurance $800 each.

Now, simply calculate the adjusted trial balance. Does it balance? Of course it does!

Journalizing Adjustments to the Trial Balance

Now we need to enter these adjustments into the general journal. Refer to the end of Chapter 6 for help. Look at Figure 9.8. How did you do? Now that the adjustments have been journalized, it is time to begin work on the financial statements.

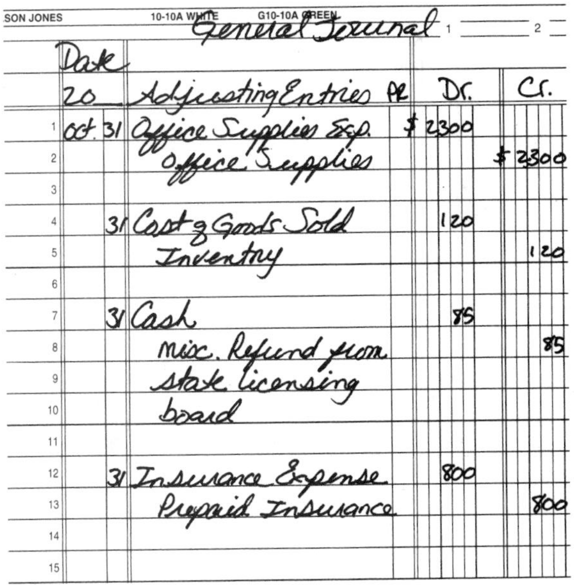

Date		Adjusting Entries	PR	Dr.	Cr.
20					
Oct.	31	Office Supplies Exp.		$ 2300	
		Office Supplies			$ 2300
	31	Cost of Goods Sold		120	
		Inventory			120
	31	Cash		85	
		misc. Refund from state licensing board			85
	31	Insurance Expense		800	
		Prepaid Insurance			800

Figure 9.8

PREPARING THE FINANCIAL STATEMENTS

This business will be using a fiscal year rather than a calendar year. The fiscal year will run from August 1 through July 31 each year. The financial statements we are preparing are for the first quarter of operations. B. Grimes will be using this data to help make managerial decisions with respect to the business.

Preparing the Income Statement

We will use the worksheet to build the income statement. Remember, we simply take the information in columns 7 and 8 from the work sheet and put it on the income statement (Figure 9.9). Did Grimes make any money in its first quarter?

Grimes Automotive Parts and Repair Shop
Income Statement
For the quarter ending October 31, 20__

Revenues		
Sales Revenue	$45,950	
Service Revenue	64,450	
Total Revenues		$110,400
Expenses		
Wages, Clerk	$5,105	
Wages, Mechanics	26,050	
Rent	9,800	
Advertising Expense	10,650	
Insurance Expense	1,200	
Office Expense	2,300	
Cost of Goods Sold	25,370	
Miscellaneous Exp.	3,260	
Total Expenses		$83,735
Net Income		$26,665

Figure 9.9

Preparing the Balance Sheet

The balance sheet is made up from columns 9 and 10 on the worksheet. Remember that owner's equity is affected by the net income or loss the business experiences during the period. In this case we have observed a net income, so owner's equity will be increased by that amount. There is one more thing that must be done before we record the owner's equity on the balance sheet. We need to subtract any withdrawals made by the owner for personal use. In summary, we will add net income to owner's equity, then subtract the withdrawals (drawing account). The answer will be reported on the balance sheet. Simply transfer that information to the balance sheet (Figure 9.10).

Your completed worksheet should look like Figure 9.11.

CLOSING THE BOOKS

To prepare our books for next quarter, we need to zero several accounts. They must be zeroed because if they are not, they will give a false picture of the business's operations. For example, if we carried a balance of $5,000 in our revenue account to a new period, at the end of that period our revenue would be overstated by $5,000. At the same time, we would have errantly understated the previous period's revenues by the same amount. If this error were not caught, management would most likely try to figure out why they had done so much more profitably this period than last. They might spend a great deal of effort looking for the improvement or simply pat themselves on the back for a job well done, even though that is not actually the case.

Grimes Automotive Parts and Repair
Balance Sheet
October 31, 20__

Assets			Liabilities		
Current Assets			Current Liabilities		
Cash	$142,285		Accounts Payable	$ 0	
Inventory	6,680		Wages Payable	0	
Supplies	5,200		Total Current Liabilities		$ 0
Total Current Assets		$154,165			
Capital Assets			Long-Term Liabilities		
Tools & Equip.	$10,500				
Total Capital Assets		$10,500	Total Long-Term Liabilities		$ 0
			Total Liabilities		$ 0
			Owner's Equity		$164,665
Total Assets		$164,665	Total Liabilities And Owner's Equity		$164,665

Figure 9.10

Zero the Revenue Accounts

Revenue accounts normally have a credit balance. You will *debit* each account to add up to the same amount as the credit balance, which will cause the balance to become zero. If we *debit* the revenue account, we must *credit* some other account. Do you know which one? See Figure 9.12 on page 83.

Zero the Expense Accounts

Expense accounts normally have a debit balance. You will credit them by the same amount as the debit balance, which will cause the balance to become zero. Just as with the revenue account above, the correcting entry is made in the income summary account. However, here we will *debit* the income summary. See Figure 9.13 on page 83.

N JONES 10-10A WHITE G10-10A GREEN

Grimes Automotive Parts and Repair Shop

October 31, 20__

Acct. No.	Account Name	Unadj. Trial Bal. Dr.	Unadj. Trial Bal. Cr.	Adjustments Dr.	Adjustments Cr.	Adj. Trial Bal. Dr.	Adj. Trial Bal. Cr.	Income Statement Dr.	Income Statement Cr.	Balance Sheet Dr.	Balance Sheet Cr.
10	Cash	$142200		$ 85	(c)	$142285				$142285	
12	Inventory	6800			(b)$ 120	6680				6680	
13	Office Supplies	7500			(a) 2300	5200				5200	
15	Tools & Equipment	10500				10500				10500	
16	Prepaid Rent										
17	Prepaid Insurance	800			(d) 800						
20	Accounts Payable										
21	Salaries Payable										
30	Owner's Equity		$150000				$150000				$150000
31	B. Grimes, Drawing	12000				12000				12000	
40	Sales Revenue		45950				45950		$45950		
41	Service Revenue		64450				64450		64450		
51	Office Supplies Exp.			2300	(a)	2300		$ 2300			
52	Rent Expense	9800				9800		9800			
53	Advertising Expense	10650				10650		10650			
54	Insurance Expense	400		800	(d)	1200		1200			
55	Wages, Clerk	5105				5105		5105			
56	Wages, Mechanic	26050				26050		26050			
57	Cost of Goods Sold	25250		120	(b)	25370		25370			
58	Misc.	3345		(c)	85	3260		3260			
	Total	$260400	$260400			$260400	$260400	$83735	$110400	$176665	$150000
	Net Income							$26665			$26665

Figure 9.11

General Journal

Date 20			Dr.	Cr.
1	Oct. 31	Sales Revenue	$45950	
2		Service Revenue	64450	
3		Income Summary		$10900
4				

Figure 9.12

General Journal

Date 20			Dr.	Cr.
1	Oct. 31	Income Summary	$83735	
2		Office Supplies Exp.		$ 2300
3		Rent Expense		9800
4		Advertising Exp.		10650
5		Insurance Exp.		1200
6		Wages, Clerk Exp.		5105
7		Wages, Mechanic Exp.		26050
8		Cost of Goods Sold Exp.		25370
9		Misc. Expense		3260
10				

Figure 9.13

General Journal

Date 20			Dr.	Cr.
1	Oct. 31	Income Summary	$12000	
2		Owner's Drawing		$12000
3				

Figure 9.14

Balance the Income Summary and the Owner's Equity Account

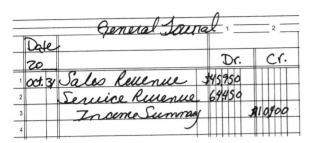

Remember, if the business made a profit, it will have a credit balance in the income summary account. If there is a debit balance, the firm has lost money in this period. If there is a credit balance, we will *debit* the income summary by the same amount and *credit* the owner's equity account. If there was a loss, we will do the opposite. What did we need to do? See Figure 9.14.

Adjust the Owner's Drawing Account

We will *credit* the drawing account by the amount of its debit balance and *debit* the owner's equity account by the same amount.

Obtain a Post-Closing Trial Balance

Finally, we obtain one last balance. Does it balance? It should!

SUMMARY

This chapter was a narrated walk through a simplified bookkeeping situation. In this chapter you posted entries that were previously made in the general journal. You should have witnessed the importance of carefully posting the entries because of their similarities and repetition. You calculated the balances on the different ledger accounts and then obtained a trial balance. You made adjustments to the trial balance and some journal entries, using the lesson on how to document adjustments. The next step was to obtain an adjusted trial balance. Then you prepared the financial reports. Finally, you prepared to close the books by zeroing the revenue account, expense account, and the drawing account. You transferred the balance from the income summary account into the owner's equity account and made closing entries in the general journal. And, in the end, the post-closing trial balance balanced!

CHAPTER 10

MERCHANDISING ACCOUNTS

KEY TERMS

service organizations, sales organizations, wholesalers, retailers, cost of goods sold, operating margin, inventory, FIFO, LIFO

Most small businesses are in one of two categories, service or sales. *Service organizations* are businesses that provide a service rather than a tangible product for their customers. Businesses such as beauty shops, bookkeeping or accounting firms, Web design and hosting organizations, and real estate firms are examples of service organizations. *Sales organizations* are businesses that sell tangible products to their consumers. Businesses such as hardware stores, grocery stores, and car dealerships are examples of sales organizations. *Wholesalers* are organizations that purchase goods directly from the manufacturer and sell them to retailers. *Retailers* are firms that buy goods at wholesale and sell them to consumers; they maintain a stock, or inventory, of goods for sale and are also called merchandisers. However, the categories may overlap, as service firms may sell some goods and retailers may provide some services. But the discussion in this chapter pertains to the retail aspect of any firm. Certain journal entries and calculations are primarily performed in merchandising operations: sales returns, purchase discounts, and inventory.

The bookkeeper for a merchandising firm must compute the cost of goods sold as part of the income statement. *Cost of goods sold* is the total cost to manufacture or to procure items that were sold at retail. Goods returned must also be accounted for. Gross (total) Revenues minus Returns equals Net Sales, or Net Customer Purchases. A simplified income statement for a merchandising firm's calculations to this point is shown in Figure 10.1.

Income Statement
For the month ending
December 31, 20__

Revenue	
Gross Sales	$85,000
Less Sales Returns	625
Net sales	$84,375
Less Cost of Goods Sold	33,050
Gross Profit on Sales	$51,325

Figure 10.1

The gross profit figure is used to calculate the operating margin of the business. *Operating margin* is used as a guide to set pricing and is computed by dividing the gross profit on sales by the gross sales. The result will be the percentage by which goods must be marked up to cover their actual cost. However, the income statement at this point does not account for stock remaining on hand for sale (*inventory*), which must be added back in (reducing profit) to determine gross profit. This is an important factor. Since we have not sold the remaining inventory, it must count against us when we are determining our profit. The remaining expenses of the business are then totaled and deducted in the usual fashion to arrive at the net income.

INVENTORY

In determining the value of inventory at the end of an accounting period, the amount on hand at the beginning must be known, the value of goods purchased during the accounting period must be added, and the value of goods sold or shipped back must be subtracted.

Figure 10.2 shows how adjustments for inventory and returns are made in calculating the cost of goods sold. Note that a value must be assigned to the inventory in order to make this computation.

Beginning Inventory		$52,000
Purchases	$28,500	
Less Purchase Returns	500	
Net Purchases		$28,000
Merchandise Available for Sale		$80,000
Less Ending Inventory		46,950
Cost of Goods Sold		$33,050

Figure 10.2

Computing the Value of Inventory

The inventory value is computed by counting the goods and then assigning a value to them. Sometimes an actual physical count is done only at the end of the year or quarter. Interim counts are approximated from records of purchase and sale. (Computer programs can be designed to accomplish this.) Bar codes on UPC labels are often used to track the sale of items and adjust the computerized inventory of that item. Physical inventory (counting items and adding up price tags) helps determine how much is being lost through shoplifting or employee pilferage and provides a check of the accuracy of the accounting records. Goods may be valued at wholesale cost or at the retail price. Often both calculations are performed.

Wholesale Value

The cost of the same goods can vary over an accounting period and with the size of orders. Suppose 25 units of a given item were purchased in January at $150 each, and 15 more units were purchased in February at $165 each. What was the cost of one unit sold in March? One method is to assume that the oldest item was sold first and to price the "goods sold" at $150. This is called the FIFO method. *FIFO* is the first in/first out method of assigning wholesale value to inventory.

An alternative is to assume that the most recently purchased item (the one bought in February) was sold and to list its cost at $165. This is called the LIFO method. *LIFO* is the last in/first out method of assigning wholesale value to inventory. In large computerized operations, a shipment number that permits valuing each item at its actual cost may be used to track merchandise. For smaller firms, FIFO or LIFO estimates may suffice. Whichever method is being used (this may be dictated by tax considerations), the bookkeeper should use it consistently.

Retail Value

The firm's owners may wish to know the retail value of inventory for tax reasons, for insurance purposes, or to compute the value of the business when it is sold. If the firm customarily marks up its merchandise by the same percentage over cost (say 35 percent), the retail value can be computed by multiplying the wholesale value of the entire inventory by 1.35. If different items are marked up by different amounts, the only alternative may be to physically examine each price tag.

RETURNED GOODS

Journalizing and posting of returns was already discussed in Chapter 3. When a sale is made, sales is credited and cash is debited. It would be simple merely to reverse this process when goods are returned, debiting sales and crediting cash. This may suffice in a service business where returns do not occur regularly in business operations. In a merchandising operation, however, it is customary to have a ledger T-account called sales returns and allowances.

When a return is made, the bookkeeper *debits* the sales and allowances account and *credits* cash or accounts receivable, depending on whether the sale was a cash or a charge transaction. This method shows management the value of goods with which the customers were dissatisfied. Sales returns are a "contra account" that works against the sales account and is ultimately subtracted from it.

PURCHASE DISCOUNTS

As already discussed in Chapter 3, purchase discounts are reductions in price that vendors offer merchandising firms for quantity orders or for prompt payment. To show discounts gained, the bookkeeper must establish a ledger T-account for purchase discounts. When a discount is taken on a transaction, the bookkeeper *debits* accounts payable, *credits* cash, and *credits* purchase discounts.

	Purchase Discounts Ledger		
20__		Dr.	Cr.
March 31	Accounts Payable	$2,000	
	Purchase Discounts		$200
	Cash		1,800

Figure 10.3

FINALIZING THE INCOME STATEMENT

Once all adjustments for inventory and returns have been made, operating expenses are entered, and the income statement is completed as it would be for a service business (Figure 10.4).

SUMMARY

In this chapter you were exposed to accounts used in merchandising or sales operations. You were introduced to new terms, inventory and items on hand for sale. There are several ways to determine the value of inventory; the two most common are FIFO and LIFO. The valuation of the inventory is important because this is part of determining the cost of goods sold. We all have returned items to the store, but we probably did not think about the effect this may have on the business. The sales returns and allowances account provides valuable information to management: the extent of customer dissatisfaction. In this chapter you

Betty's Bootery
Income Statement
Year ended December 31, 20__

Revenue			
Gross Sales			$85,000
Less Sales Returns and Allowances			625
Net Sales			$84,375
Expenses			
Beginning Inventory 1/1/__		$52,000	
Purchases	$28,500		
Less Purchase Returns	500		
Net Purchases		$28,000	
Merchandise Available for Sale		$80,000	
Less Inventory 12/31/__		46,950	
Cost of Goods Sold			33,050
Gross Profit on Sales			$51,325
Operating Expenses			
Rent Expense		$10,000	
Wages and Salaries Expense		10,000	
Utilities Expense		3,000	
Supplies Expense		1,000	
Advertising Expense		1,000	
Total Expenses			$25,000
Net Income			$26,325

Figure 10.4

learned about a new kind of account called a contra account, which works against the asset account. In this case, the sales return account is the contra account to the sales account. You also learned how to account for purchase discounts.

CHAPTER 11 DEPRECIATION

KEY TERMS

fixed assets, depreciation, book value, salvage value, accelerated depreciation, straight-line depreciation, sum-of-years-digits method, double declining balance method, units of production method

In the discussion of assets in Chapter 1, two kinds of assets were described: current assets and capital assets. *Capital assets,* also called fixed assets, include land and buildings, furniture and fixtures, vehicles, machinery, and equipment. (Together they are sometimes listed as *property, plant,* and *equipment.*)

WHAT IS DEPRECIATION?

Fixed assets are items that are not for sale; they are used in operating the business. Because they last a long time, their cost cannot logically be charged to the year in which they are purchased. But because fixed assets do wear out or become obsolete, their decline in useful value must be accounted for (and money for replacement must be budgeted). This is done by spreading their cost over their useful life and deducting a part of that cost each year as depreciation expense. *Depreciation* is the reduction in value of an asset as it is used.

To determine the value of a piece of equipment at any time of its life and also to determine the total current value of fixed assets when computing the balance sheet, two accounts are needed: depreciation expense, which becomes part of the operating expenses, and accumulated depreciation, which is a contra asset account charged against assets.

A journal entry for depreciation expense is a *debit* to the depreciation expense account and a *credit* to the accumulated depreciation account. Any reduction to an asset is considered an expense; however, no movement of cash or writing of a check is required for depreciation expense. The amounts must be transferred from *depreciation schedules* on which the calculations are made. (See Figure 11.1.)

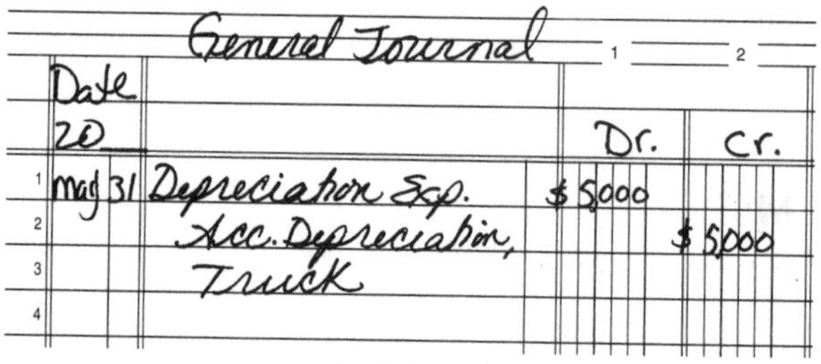

Figure 11.1

Although calculations of depreciation are made in terms of years, depreciation expense is deducted monthly, so the yearly figure must be divided by 12. If an asset is purchased during the first half of the month, a whole month's depreciation is customarily taken. If an item is purchased after the fifteenth of the month, depreciation might be ignored for that month and deductions would begin the following month.

The *book value* is the current depreciated value of an asset (or of all assets except land) and is determined by subtracting its accumulated depreciation from its cost. For example, if your firm purchased a truck for $35,000, and its accumulated depreciation was $5,000, it would appear on the capital assets section of the balance sheet as shown in Figure 11.2.

Balance Sheet

Capital Assets		
Truck	$35,000	
Accumulated Depreciation	5,000	
Total Capital Assets		$30,000

Figure 11.2

If a firm owns many fixed assets, they are often grouped by category on the balance sheet, although records are maintained for the individual pieces of equipment—buildings, vehicles, office equipment, machine tools, and so on. Land is put into a separate category because land does not depreciate.

METHODS OF CALCULATING DEPRECIATION

In figuring depreciation, several factors are taken into account:

- The original cost of the asset
- Its estimated useful lifetime in years
- Its estimated salvage value

Salvage value is the trade-in value or estimated selling price at the end of an asset's useful life. It is not possible to determine exactly how long an asset will be useful, so some flexibility is tolerated. The IRS can provide guidelines suggesting the useful lives of different kinds of equipment.

There are four options available in calculating depreciation:

1. The straight-line method
2. The double declining balance method
3. The sum-of-years-digits method
4. The units of production method, (which is mainly used for manufacturing equipment)

The sum-of-years-digits and double declining balance methods yield accelerated depreciation. *Accelerated depreciation* is where the greatest proportion of the expense is taken in the first year, with successively smaller amounts being taken in later years. The method chosen is generally a management decision determined by tax or other considerations.

The Straight-Line Method

Straight-line depreciation is the simplest to compute. *Straight-line depreciation* is where the salvage value is deducted from the cost and the remaining amount is divided by the estimated useful life of the asset. Suppose your firm purchased a truck that cost $35,000 and was expected to last for five years, and it would be worth $2,500 at trade-in. Your annual depreciation would be as shown in the equation:

$$\frac{\$35{,}000 - \$2{,}500}{5 \text{ years}} = \$6{,}500$$

Since depreciation expense is generally charged monthly, you would divide $6,500 by 12.

Each month you would *debit* depreciation expense and *credit* accumulated depreciation by $541.67 until the entire $35,000 had been accounted for.

The Sum-of-Years-Digits Method

The *sum-of-years-digits* is the method of depreciation that uses a calculation in which a fraction, whose numerator (top number in a fraction) consists of the remaining years of the expected lifetime and the denominator (bottom number in a fraction) is the sum of all the years of life. For example, for an asset expected to last five years, you would add:

5 + 4 + 3 + 2 + 1 = 15

Your denominator would be 15. In the first year you would have a depreciation expense of 5/15ths of the cost (less salvage value), and so on:

5/15ths × original cost minus trade-in = 1st year depreciation

4/15ths × original cost minus trade-in = 2nd year depreciation

3/15ths × original cost minus trade-in = 3rd year depreciation

2/15ths × original cost minus trade-in = 4th year depreciation

1/15th × original cost minus trade-in = 5th year depreciation

Let's look at the same truck scenario.

$35,000 − $2,500 = $32,500 (This will be our basis.)

5/15ths × 32,500 = $10,833.33 for the 1st year depreciation

4/15ths × 32,500 = $8,666.67 for the 2nd year depreciation

3/15ths × 32,500 = $6,500.00 for the 3rd year depreciation

2/15ths × 32,500 = $4,333.33 for the 4th year depreciation

1/15th × 32,500 = $2,166.67 for the 5th year depreciation

All five years totaled equals $32,500.00.

Double Declining Balance Method

Like the sum-of-years-digits method, the *double declining balance method* is an accelerated method of depreciation where the residual (salvage) value is ignored until the end. The percentage of depreciation taken each year is based on the straight-line rate multiplied by two. For example, straight-line depreciation of an asset with an estimated life of five years would be 20 percent per year. Multiplied by two, this gives 40 percent of the asset value. That amount is deducted in the first year, and the remaining value of the asset is then multiplied by 40 percent to determine the second year's depreciation, and so on.

Year	Undepreciated value at beginning of year	Depreciation of asset	Value remaining at year's end
1	$35,000	$14,000	$21,000
2	21,000	8,400	12,600
3	12,600	5,040	7,560
4	7,560	3,024	4,536
5	4,536	1,814	2,722

The final value is adjusted so that the final book value equals the residual (salvage) value that was estimated at the outset. In the foregoing example, the total depreciation taken comes to $32,278. When subtracted from $35,000, this leaves $2,722, which is considered the residual value. Since the residual value should be $2,500, we will be allowed to take the additional $222 in the final year, meaning that year five's depreciation expense will be $2,036 instead of the calculated $1,814.

Units of Production Method

Some machines become less useful as they are used. For example, the usefulness of an automobile is more a function of miles traveled than of age. The formula for the *units of production method* consists of first deducting the salvage value and then dividing the purchase price by the number of units thought to be the best indicator of usefulness (for example, mileage or hours of operation). Suppose a die mold used to stamp out steel parts was estimated to be capable of stamping out 4,000 parts before becoming useless. It cost $81,000, and its salvage value is estimated to be $1000. It stamped a total of 1,000 units in the current year, so:

$$\frac{\$81{,}000 - \$1{,}000}{4{,}000} \times 1{,}000 = \$20{,}000 \text{ (depreciation)}$$

As with the double declining balance method, the final value in the above calculation would be adjusted to equal the residual value that was originally estimated.

SUMMARY

Assets do not last forever. As an asset ages or is utilized, it retains less value than when it was new. The term book value is given to describe the value of an asset less its accumulated depreciation. A business must account for this change in value; depreciation is the method for doing so. Four different methods of calculating depreciation are accelerated depreciation, straight-line, double declining balance, and sum-of-years-digits method. Each of these methods produces a different result at the different stages of depreciation. Even though this is the case, they all will produce the same final value for the asset. The largest factors in determining the method of depreciation are the type of asset and the tax implication on the business.

EXERCISES

11.1 Use the straight-line method to compute the first year's depreciation and then the first monthly depreciation expense for a $3,900 computer printer with an expected life of three years and a trade-in value of $300.

11.2 Using the sum-of-years-digits method, calculate the depreciation for each of the three years of life of the computer printer described in Exercise 11.1.

11.3 Now use the double declining balance method to calculate the annual depreciation for the computer printer described in Exercise 11.1.

11.4 Suppose the computer printer described in the foregoing examples has an expected life of 10,000 hours and worked for 2,000 hours this year. Compute this year's depreciation.

ANSWERS

11.1 $1,200 per year depreciation, first month depreciation is $100.

$3,900 − $300 = $3,600 is the basis for the depreciation.

Divide $3,600 by 3 (number of years) to calculate the annual depreciation.

Then divide the annual depreciation by the number of months in a year giving you the first month's depreciation expense. $1,200 ÷ 12 = $100 per month.

11.2 First year, $1,800 depreciation.

Second year, $1,200.

Third year, $600.

The basis is the same as above. The sum of the years is 6 (1 + 2 + 3 = 6); this will be the denominator in our fraction. The numerator is the years remaining. First year 3/6ths × $3,600 = $1,800. Second year 2/6ths × $3,600 = $1,200. Third year 1/6th × $3,600 = $600.

11.3 First year, $2,600 depreciation.

Second year, $867.

Third year, $133.

Residual value is ignored in this method until the final year. Look at straight-line depreciation first (1/3rd if the asset is depreciated each year) to determine how much depreciation we will get each year.

Double the value of the straight-line method so we will be depreciating 2/3rds of the asset's remaining value each year.

First year, 2/3rds × $3,900 = $2,600.

Second year, 2/3rds × $1,300 = $867.

Third year, 2/3rds × $433 = $289. This would cause the depreciated value to fall below the residual value, which is not allowed. So we look at the residual value of $300 which is subtracted from the $433 value at the end of the second year and see that our third year's depreciation expense is $133.

11.4 $720

$3,900 − $300 = $3,600

2,000 hours ÷ 10,000 hours = .2

$3,600 × .2 = $720

CHAPTER 12

CHECKING ACCOUNTS

KEY TERMS

negotiable instrument, drawer, payee, drawee, check register, bank statement, bank reconciliation

A *negotiable instrument* is a written promise of one person to pay a specific sum of money to another person either on demand or at a certain date in the future. The type of negotiable instrument most commonly encountered in bookkeeping is a check. Promissory notes, which are also negotiable instruments, are discussed in Chapter 14.

HOW CHECKS ARE USED

A check is a written instrument that is signed by the depositor of a demand account (checking account) ordering the bank to pay a specified amount to a designated person. Three parties are involved:

- The *drawer* is the person or business that creates the check and signs it on its face (the front).
- The *payee* is the person or business that receives the check and must endorse (sign) it on the back to cash or deposit it.
- The *drawee* is the bank on which the face amount (the sum for which the check is written) is drawn.

Business checks, available from commercial banks or specialized suppliers, are prenumbered in sequence and have stubs or vouchers on which to record the date drawn, the amount, the payee's name, and the purpose of the check.

The Check Register

A *check register* is a running record of all checks written, deposits made, interest earned, and bank charges or fees imposed on a checking account. Some kind of running record must be kept by subtracting the amount of each check from the balance, subtracting any additional charges to the account such as bank service charges, and adding any deposit made to the account (as well as interest if the account is interest-bearing). A check register may be supplied for this purpose, or the check stubs may be used.

Supporting Documents

Each check that is written requires a supporting document such as a vendor's invoice, a utility bill, or a payroll summary. In the case of checks that are written for petty cash purposes (see Chapter 13), a supporting document in the form of a memo should be created, approved, signed, and dated. (Preprinted forms for this purpose are available at stationery stores.)

When a check is written, the supporting document should be marked "paid" on its face, with the date and check number noted.

A rubber stamp designed for this purpose is convenient. Marking the document as paid reduces the chance that the same bill will be paid twice and makes it easier to locate the correct check if a question occurs about payment. Paid bills should be removed from the unpaid bill folder and filed in a paid-bill file.

Deposits made to the checking account are accompanied by a deposit slip. You retain a copy and the bank retains one or more copies for its records.

Bank Statements

At specified intervals, usually monthly, the bank will send the checking account holder a bank statement. A *bank statement* indicates all activity in a bank account for the month. Specifically, the statement will show

- The depositor's beginning balance
- Additions caused by deposits (credits)
- Interest, if any (credits)
- Deductions caused by checks that have been paid out by the bank (that is, checks that have "cleared")
- Bank charges such as service charges, new checks, charges for use of automatic teller (ATM) machines

For routine charges such as account-service charges, banks do not usually issue supporting documents, but for items such as check printing, returned-check (overdraft) charges, stop-payment charges, and the like, the bank will send the depositor a debit memo.

The checks that have been received and paid by the bank (canceled checks) are returned with the statement. (These will usually not include all checks written during the statement period.) Additionally, some banks offer online checking and electronically post the canceled checks so they may be viewed over the Internet. Copies of deposit slips will also be returned. The bookkeeper uses the bank statement, the canceled checks, and the deposit slips to prepare the bank reconciliation.

RECONCILING THE CHECKING ACCOUNT

As already suggested, the running balance in the check register and the final balance shown on the bank statement are not likely to agree. Some bank charges may not have been recorded (since they cannot be known until they appear on the statement); some checks may not have cleared because of delays in reaching the bank; and some deposits may not yet have credited. The *bank reconciliation* is prepared to verify the accuracy of the bank's records and the firm's checking account register. The bank can make an error! If we have accurate records we can ensure that all charges are correct.

Rigorous monthly reconciliation of the bank statement is critical to effective bookkeeping. Among its purposes is the prevention or discovery of embezzlement. For this reason, reconciliation is best performed by someone other than the person who issues the checks.

The steps in reconciling a bank statement are as follows:

1. Add up the amounts recorded in the past month's check stubs and compare these with the total for the month in the cash payments journal.

2. Sort the canceled checks into numerical order and compare each returned check with its check stub and with the bank statement. Check off the returned checks on the check register or stub and on the statement. List any that have not been returned, total them, and label this amount "checks not cleared."

3. Add up the month's deposit slips and compare the amount with (*a*) the total deposits recorded on the check stubs, (*b*) the total in the cash receipts journal, and (*c*) the total shown on the bank statement.

4. Note and add up any deposits not listed on the bank statement; label these "deposits in transit."

5. Look at the bank statement's balance of your account; *add* deposits in transit, *subtract* checks not cleared, *add* or *subtract* any bank errors, and label the resulting sum "adjusted bank balance."

6. To your check register total, *add* any additions (such as interest) made to your account by the bank, *subtract* any bank charges, *add* or *subtract* any depositor's errors, and label the resultant sum "adjusted balance."

Your adjusted balance and the adjusted bank balance should agree. If they do not, you will have to find the error and adjust your records accordingly. This work is generally done on a bank reconciliation form like the one illustrated in Figure 12.1.

Tutor/Tape Corporation
Bank Reconciliation
September 30, 20__

Balance according to bank statement		$______
Plus any additions or deposits not on bank statement ("in transit")	$______	
Minus checks issued but not yet cleared by the bank ("outstanding checks")	______	
Plus or minus any bank errors	______	
Adjusted bank balance		$______
Bank balance according to depositor's records		$______
Plus any interest or addition by the bank not recorded in depositor's records	$______	
Minus bank charges, monthly fees not recorded by depositor	______	
Plus or minus any depositor errors	______	
Adjusted balance		$______

Figure 12.1

RECORDING ADJUSTMENTS TO THE CHECKING ACCOUNT

Any adjustments made to the checking account must be entered into the check register as well as the journals. For example, if a check was recorded in an amount smaller than the face amount, the difference is a *credit* to cash and is entered in the cash payments journal with an explanation. The check register must also be corrected. If the check was recorded for more than its face amount, the adjustment is entered in brackets [$12.00] to show that this is a negative amount to be debited to the cash account.

Journal entries for bank service charges and for amounts collected by the bank are shown in Figure 12.2.

Journal

	Date			1	2
	20			Dr.	Cr.
1	Oct.	1	Cash	$ 15	
2			Bank service charge		$ 15
3					
4		1	Cash		
5			Note Receivable, Jones	1,250	
6			Note collected by		1,250
7			bank		
8					

Figure 12.2

SUMMARY

Business checking accounts are not all that different from personal accounts. In this chapter you were given some new terms such as drawer, payee, and drawee. These terms are used to clarify who is paying whom and how (what financial institution is involved). We discussed supporting documentation, which includes invoices, bills, and memos. Bank statements were discussed, as well as how to reconcile (balance) the bank's records with the business's records. You were also shown the procedure for recording this information as well as any adjustments that have been made.

CHAPTER 13 HANDLING PETTY CASH

KEY TERMS

petty cash fund, imprest fund, petty cash voucher, petty cash journal

Although business payments should be made by check whenever possible, it is not always practical to do so. A check may not be acceptable in some situations (for example, for a taxi or bus fare), or no check may be available when an expenditure is made. A *petty cash fund* is a fund established for the payment of small cash expenses. To meet the need for small cash payments, the bookkeeper may set up a petty cash fund.

THE PETTY CASH FUND

To establish a petty cash fund, a small amount of cash (say $200) is set aside for this purpose. The money may be kept in a locked petty cash box with one person being held responsible for it. No bookkeeping entry is needed when the cash is drawn since the petty cash fund together with the cash in the bank accounts equals the cash owned by the business. This kind of advance of money is called an imprest fund. An *imprest fund* is advanced (lent) money. A memorandum record of it is made, but it requires no posting to the ledger. For an active petty cash fund with frequent withdrawals, a special journal may be created.

Removals of cash from the fund must be supported by either a receipt (Figure 13.1) or a petty cash voucher. The *petty cash voucher* is a slip or form recording who received the money, the date, and the purpose of the expenditure; it may be signed or initialed by the person responsible for the petty cash fund. The key to this is consistency; do it the same way all of the time. Stationers and office supply stores carry printed cash forms.

PETTY CASH RECEIPT

Number: 24 Date: May 5, 2006

Paid to: Postmaster

For: postage due

Amount: $.37

Received payment: a. Carrier Approved by: A. M.

Figure 13.1

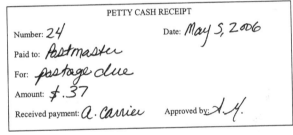

At the end of the month, the receipts and vouchers are totaled and the remaining cash is counted. The total of receipts and vouchers plus the remaining cash must always equal the established amount.

When the cash fund runs low, it must be brought back up to the established sum. Upon verifying the total of the receipts, the bookkeeper issues a check in that amount to the order of petty cash. Receipts are posted to the cash payments journal in order to *credit* cash and *debit* the appropriate expense accounts.

Company Name

ON JONES 10-10A WHITE G10-10A GREEN

Petty Cash Journal March 20__

Date 20__		Description	Receipts	Payments Cr.	Office Exp. Dr.	Del. Exp. Dr.	Postage Exp. Dr.	Sales Exp. Dr.
Mar.	1	Check No. 514	$ 100					
	5	Stamps		$ 12 50			$ 12 50	
	6	Oil		4 10		$ 4 10		
	12	Stationary		9 40	$ 7 40			
	15	Bulbs		4 00	4 00			
	18	Sales Lunch		24 50				$ 24 50
	20	Taxi		8 00				8 00
	28	Tape		5 00	5 00			
				$ 67 50	$ 18 40	$ 4 10	$ 12 50	$ 32 50
				(11)	(51)	(54)	(57)	(59)

Figure 13.2

THE PETTY CASH JOURNAL

When there is an active petty cash fund for which detailed or frequent records are required, a special petty cash journal may be set up. The *petty cash journal* is used to record all transactions to a petty cash fund. To open the petty cash account, a check is drawn to petty cash and entered in this special journal. Payments to petty cash are entered as shown in Figure 13.2. At the end of the month, the totals are posted as a *debit* to each individual expense account and a *credit* to petty cash.

SUMMARY

In this chapter you learned that some small transactions must be handled using cash. The use of this cash is formalized in something called a petty cash fund. Whenever cash is removed from the petty cash fund, a voucher or receipt supporting the expenditure must be left in its place. This record keeping is very important and is often accomplished by someone with little or no bookkeeping experience. Since this is the case, the procedures should be simple and clearly defined. An active petty cash account may require the establishment of a special petty cash journal.

CHAPTER 14

INTEREST

KEY TERMS

interest, principal, interest rate, time, promissory note, discounted note, maturity

Interest is rent charged for the use of money. Most lending institution transactions involve interest in some form. Bookkeeping for businesses also involves working with interest. Your firm may charge interest on past-due accounts and may hold promissory notes (signed promises to pay a certain sum by a certain date) from customers. Suppliers and creditors may charge the firm interest, and the firm may have loans or mortgages for equipment or real estate on which interest must be paid.

Interest your business pays to its creditors, including banks, is interest expense, and payments of interest are recorded as cash disbursements. They are a *credit* to the cash account and a *debit* to the interest expense account.

Interest received from customers or debtors is interest income. It is a *debit* to the cash account and a *credit* to interest income (revenue).

CALCULATING INTEREST

Three elements are used in figuring the amount of interest due on a borrowed sum of money.

- The *principal* is the amount of money borrowed.
- The *interest rate* is the amount charged for the loan, expressed as a percentage.
- The *time* is the number of months or days the principal is held by the borrower.

The interest rate, which is stated as a yearly rate, must be adjusted to the actual length of the loan. The formula for doing this is:

$$I = P\,R\,T$$

Where

I = Interest

P = Principal

R = Rate

T = Time

$$\text{Interest} = \text{Principal} \times \text{Rate} \times \text{Time}$$

$$\text{Interest} = \frac{\text{Principal}}{1} \times \frac{\text{Rate}}{100} \times \frac{\text{Time in Days}}{360}$$

In this formula, interest is given as a fraction with the rate as the numerator and 100 as the denominator. Most banks consider a year to consist of 360 days, not 365, for convenience in calculating. Therefore, in the interest equation, the time is expressed as a fraction with the number of days as the numerator and 360 as the denominator. Alternatively, 12 months may be used instead of 360 days. A 3-month (90-day) loan would thus be expressed as 3/12.

For example, the interest on $1,000 (*P*) borrowed at 12 percent (*R*) for 60 days (*T*) is calculated as follows:

$$I = \frac{\$1{,}000}{1} \times \frac{12}{100} \times \frac{60}{360}$$

$$I = \$1{,}000 \times .12 \times .1667$$

$$I = \$20$$

RECORDING INTEREST

Paid by the Business

If your firm is *paying* interest, then you enter it into the cash payments journal in connection with the loan account. Figure 14.1 shows such transactions. The ledger account to which the interest is eventually posted may be in the name of the holder of a mortgage, the holder of a note, or a vendor to whom a payment was made late.

Received by the Business

Interest is an expense when paid and a revenue when received. An interest income account is set up and credited whenever a payment of interest is received. This account represents an increase in owner's equity. The transaction is entered in the cash receipts journal as a *debit* to cash and a *credit* to interest income (See Figure 14.2).

HANDLING PROMISSORY NOTES

A *promissory note* is a written commitment by one person to pay a definite sum of money to another at a specified future date. Installment loans are a form of promissory in which payments are made periodically rather than in a lump sum. Simpler forms of promissory notes are much like checks in appearance. In current practice, however, notes and loans are more often complex documents listing not only the interest and principal, but many legal

ON JONES 10-10A WHITE G10-10A GREEN

Date 20__	Ck. No.	Payee	Explanation	Cash Cr.	Purch. Disc. Cr.	Acct. Pay. Dr.	Account	Account Dr.
Jan. 1	10	State Bank	90-day note @12%	$1010			Notes Payable	$1,000
							Interest Expense	10
2	11	Charlo Supply	Interest on 10% note	37			Interest Expense	37
3	12	Vendall Inc.	Payment of overdue acct.	203		$200	Interest Expense	3
5	13	Sharon Paper Co.	Invoice less 2%	98	$2	100		
				$1348	$2	$300		$1,050

Figure 14.1

Cash Receipts Journal

Date 20		Received from	Explanation	Cash Dr.	Sales Disc. Dr.	Accounts Rec. Cr.	Account	Account Cr.
Jan.	2	B. Morgan	Pd. on account	$2000		$2000		
	2	Smith Brothers		400		400		
	2	Sales		6200			Sales	$6200
	4	M. Platt	overdue acct.	404		400	Interest Income	4
	5	Bank	Received Interest	5				5
	12	S. Davey	60-day note w/	510			Note Receivable	500
			interest				Interest Income	10
	16	Donut Ltd.	Invoice less 2%	98	$2	100		
	17	Rick's Radiator	Interest on	600			Interest Income	600
			mortgage					
	23	P. Sunshine	30-day note w/	3018			Note Receivable	3000
			interest				Interest Income	18
	23	C. Edgars	overdue acct	803		800	Interest Income	3
			w/interest					
	31	Sales		7200			Sales	7200
				$21238	$2	$3700		$17540

Figure 14.2

conditions and terms of repayment as well. If you have taken out a car loan, for example, one of the documents you signed—the installment contract—was a form of promissory note. I am sure you noticed several legal terms on that document.

When a business firm borrows money, it issues some form of promissory note as evidence of the debt. Notes for 30, 60, or 90 days (short-term borrowing) are common in business. A record of this liability and the interest expense it incurs is set up as shown in Figure 14.3.

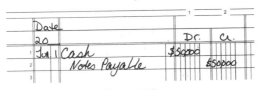

Date 20			Dr.	Cr.
Jan.	1	Cash	$50000	
		Notes Payable		$50000

Figure 14.3

When the note is paid, the journal entry is made as shown in Figure 14.4.

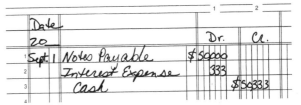

Date 20			Dr.	Cr.
Sept.	1	Notes Payable	$50000	
		Interest Expense	333	
		Cash		$50333

Figure 14.4

There is another note called a discounted note. A *discounted note* is a loan in which the interest on the note is paid in advance. For example, the firm borrows $5,000 for 30 days at 18 percent per year on a discounted note. The interest of $75 is deducted at once, and the borrower receives only $4,925, but must pay back $5,000 at maturity. *Maturity* is the date when the loan comes due (in this case, at the end of 30 days).

In the transaction shown in Figure 14.5, $10,000 was borrowed on June 1 in the form of a 90-day discounted note on which the interest was $1,000. When the note matures on

September 1 and is paid, the entry will appear as shown in Figure 14.6.

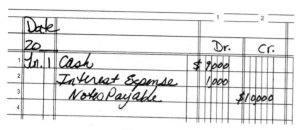

Date		Dr.	Cr.
20			
Jn. 1	Cash	$ 9000	
	Interest Expense	1000	
	Notes Payable		$10000

Figure 14.5

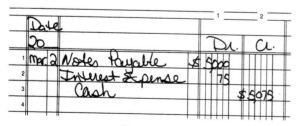

Date		Dr.	Cr.
20			
Sep. 1	Notes Payable	$10000	
	Cash		$10000

Figure 14.6

Sometimes, for example in the purchase of vehicles or equipment, a cash down payment is made, leaving a sum to be paid off. A note is signed for this balance. Suppose your firm purchases a machine costing $35,000, making a down payment of $5,000, and signing a note for $30,000 as seen in Figure 14.7.

Date		Dr.	Cr.
20			
Feb. 2	Machinery	$35000	
	Cash		$ 5000
	Notes Payable		30000

Figure 14.7

When part of this note is paid, the principal is recorded to Notes Payable and the interest to Interest Expense as seen in Figure 14.8.

Date		Dr.	Cr.
20			
Mar. 2	Notes Payable	$ 5000	
	Interest Expense	75	
	Cash		$5075

Figure 14.8

SUMMARY

Interest is rent paid for the use of money, whether you charge it to past-due creditors for the use of your money or pay it to the bank for the use of its money. You learned how to calculate interest using the formula: $I = PRT$. You were shown how to record interest received (income) and interest paid (expense). Promissory notes were described as written contracts between two parties stipulating who will pay whom a specified amount of money at a specified future date.

EXERCISES

14.1. Using the worksheet provided (Figure 14.9), enter the following transactions into the cash payments journal. Indicate the accounts to which postings would be made but do not post.

June 1: Sent check of $303 to A. North to pay 60-day note of $300 plus interest of $3.00.

June 5: Sent check of $277.75 to Gibson Company for the past due account of $275 plus interest of $2.75.

June 8: Sent check of $6,000 to Stern Company for semiannual interest due on mortgage of $100,000 at rate of 12 percent per year.

June 12: Paid note of $5,000 owed to City Bank with interest of 10 percent for 2 months ($I = PRT = \$83.33$).

June 15: Paid $360 to Arless Company for overdue account plus 6 percent interest at $1.80.

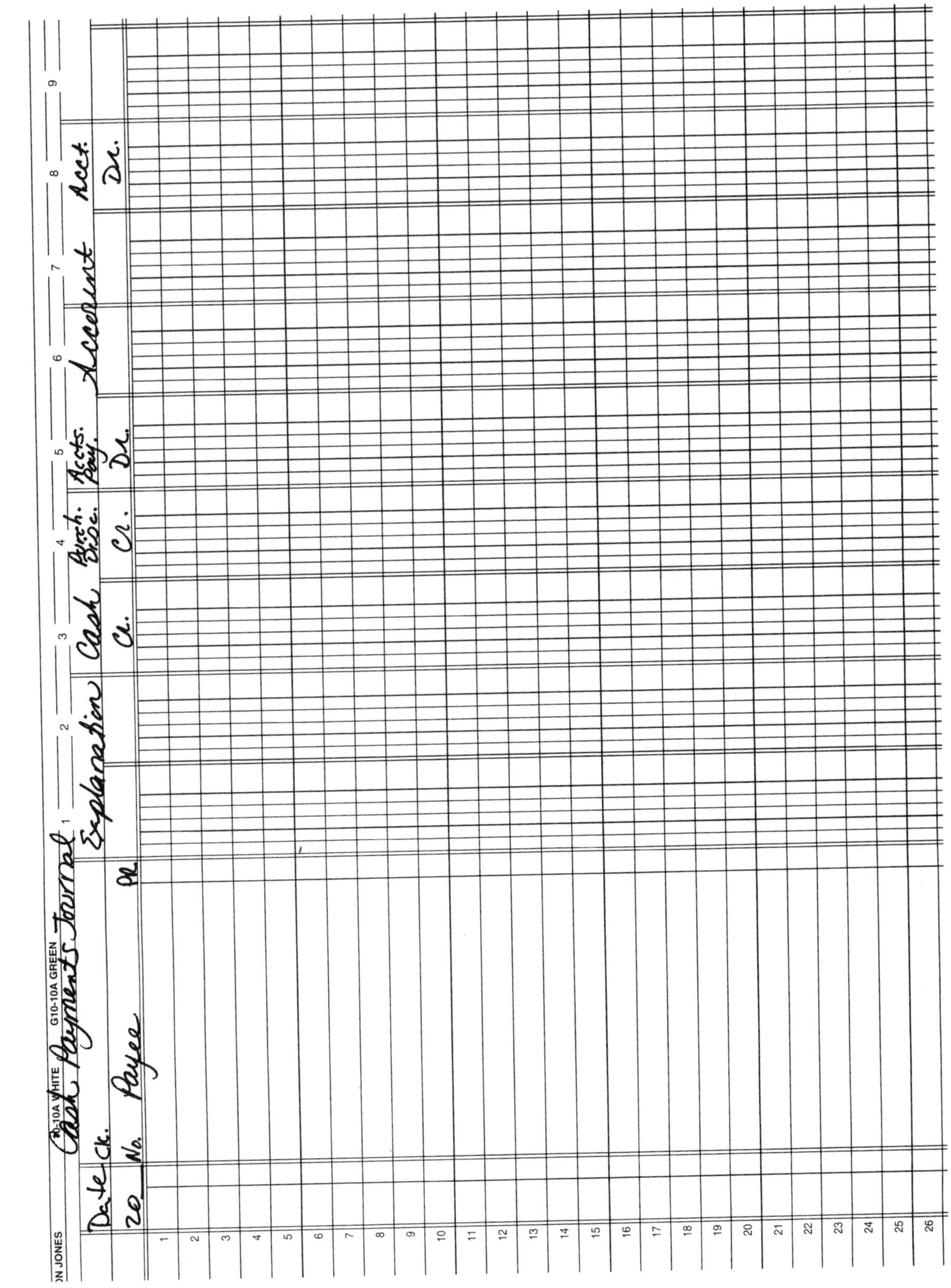
G10-10A WHITE G10-10A GREEN
Cash Payments Journal
Date
20__
Ck. No.
Payee
PR
Explanation
Cash Cr.
Purch. Disc. Cr.
Accts. Pay. Dr.
Account
Acct. Dr.

Figure 14.9

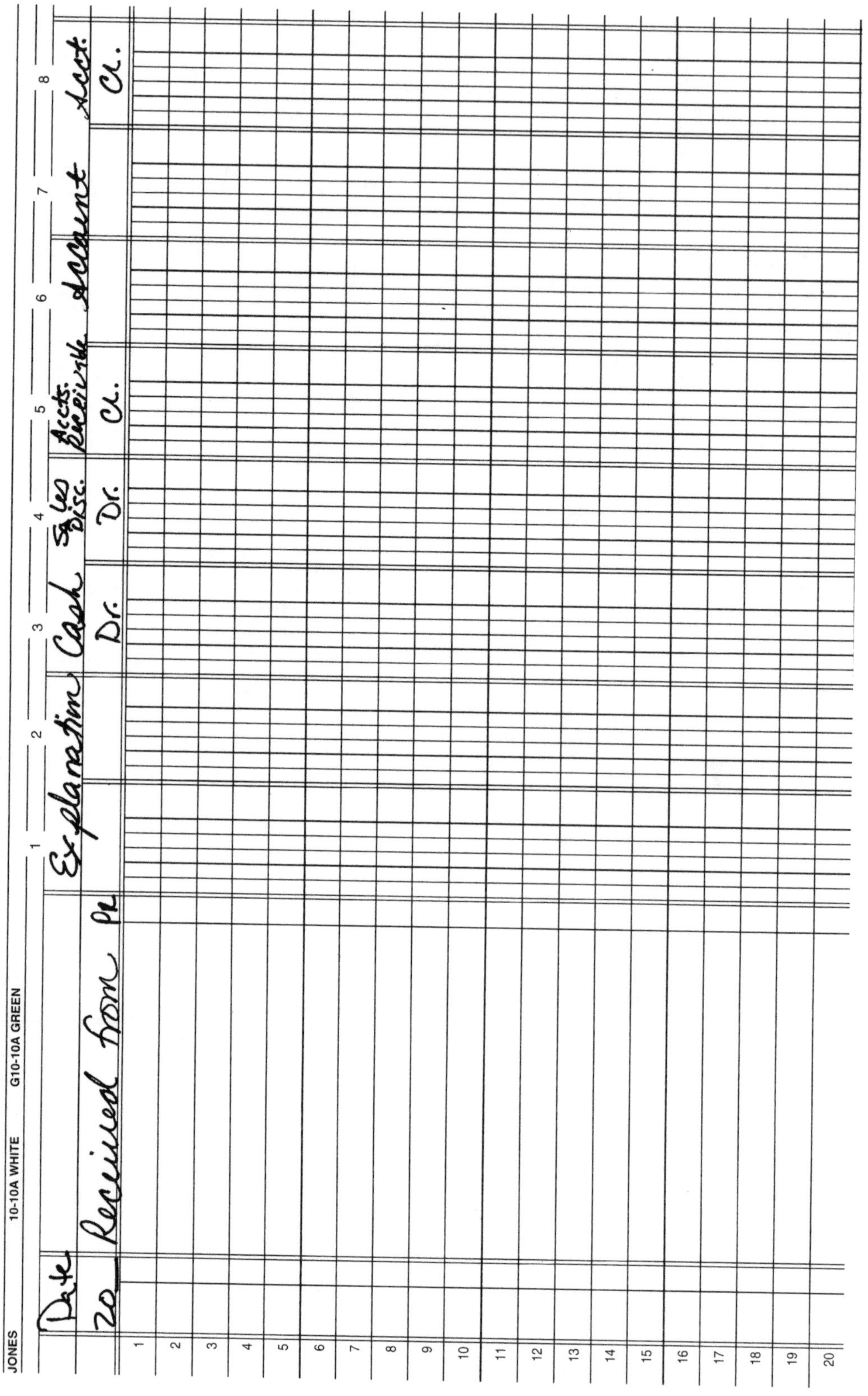
JONES
10-10A WHITE
G10-10A GREEN
Date
20__
Received from
P.R.
Explanation
Cash
Dr.
Sales Disc.
Dr.
Accts. Receivable
Cr.
Account
Acct.
Cr.

Figure 14.10

June 21: Sent check of $9,000 to Tryson Mortgage Company for quarterly interest due on mortgage of $400,000 at a rate of 9 percent per year ($I = PRT =$ $9,000).

14.2. Using the worksheet provided (Figure 14.10), enter the following into the cash receipts journal and show where the entries would be posted.

Mar. 5: Received check for $303 from L. Herbit on his overdue account of $300 plus $3.00 interest.

Mar. 8: Bank credited your firm's account with $3.00 interest on one of your accounts.

Mar. 12: L. Crane sent check for $606 for his 60-day note with principal of $600 and interest of $6.00.

Mar. 13: Received check from R. Ralston in payment of invoice of $450 less a 2 percent discount.

Mar. 15: Received check for $500 from Richards & Company in payment of monthly interest on its mortgage.

Mar. 18: Received check for $3,015 from L. Johnson for her 30-day note of $3,000 and interest.

Mar. 25: John Good paid his overdue account of $400 plus interest of $2.00.

ANSWERS

14.1 See Figure 14.9A

14.2 See Figure 14.10A

I JONES — 10-10A WHITE — G10-10A GREEN

Cash Payments Journal

Line	Date 20__		Ck. No.	Payee	P.R.	Explanation	Cash Cr.	Purch. Disc. Cr.	Accts. Pay. Dr.	Account	Acct. Dr.
1	Jun.	1	1	A. North	24	60-day 6% note	$ 303			Notes Payable	$ 300
2					56	Payable				Interest Exp.	3
3		5	2	Gibson Co.	56	Overdue acct.	277 75		$ 275	Interest Exp.	2 75
4						w/interest					
5		8	3	Stern Co.	56	Interest on	6000			Interest Exp.	6,000
6						mortg. for 6 mo.					
7		12	4	City Banks	24	2-mo. note w/	5083 33			Notes Payable	5000
8					56	10% interest				Interest Exp.	83 33
9		15	5	Arless Co.	56	Overdue acct	361 80		360	Interest Exp.	1 80
10						w/6% interest					
11		21	6	Tryson Mortg. Co.	56	Semi-annual	9000			Interest Exp.	9000
12						9% interest on	$21025 88		$ 635		$20390 88
13						mortg.	(11)		(21)		(X)
14											

Figure 14.9A

My Company
Cash Receipts Journal

N JONES   G10-10A WHITE   G10-10A GREEN

Date 20__		Received from	PR	Explanation	Cash Dr.	Sales Disc. Dr.	Accts. Receivable Cr.	Account	Acct. Cr.
Mar.	5	J. Herbit		Overdue accts	303		$ 300	Interest Income	3
	8	Bank		Interest on acct	3			Interest Income	3
	12	J. Crane		60-day note w/	606			Note Receivable	600
				Interest				Interest Income	6
	13	R. Ralston		Invoice less 2%	441	$ 9	450		
	15	Richards & Co.		Interest on	500			Interest Income	500
				matg. for 1mo.					
	18	J. Johnson		30-day note w/	3015			Note Receivable	3000
				interest				Interest Income	15
	25	John Good		Overdue acct.	402		400	Interest Income	2
				w/interest	$5270	$ 9	$ 1150		$ 4129

Figure 14.10A

CHAPTER 15 PAYROLL RECORDS

KEY TERMS

wages, salaries, gross wages, net wages, Individual Retirement Account (IRA), tax-deferred contributions, 401(k) plan, individual earnings record, payroll register, employee's individual payroll report

Payroll records keep track of wages and salaries. *Wages* are hourly compensation paid for employees; *salaries* are compensation paid to employees who are hired at a flat yearly, monthly, or (sometimes) weekly compensation.

KEEPING HOURLY RECORDS AND COMPUTING WAGES

The hours worked by salaried employees are not normally recorded. For wage earners, however, records of hours must be kept not only to compute their compensation, but also to comply with local, state, and federal wage and hour laws and (in some cases) union regulations. For example, most states and the federal government require that time and a half be paid to employees who work more than forty hours in a week. Some employee contracts specify that double the usual hourly rate be paid for work done on Sundays or holidays, and some employers pay a premium for evening or night shift work.

A time clock or an in/out log may be used to keep workers' hours. Regular wages are computed by multiplying the hourly rate by the hours worked; overtime is usually computed separately. The worker's regular wages ("straight time") plus overtime, if any, are called gross wages. *Gross wages* are the total of all wages and overtime, before taxes and other deductions have been imposed.

For salaried personnel, the gross wages for the pay period consist of the annual salary divided by the number of pay periods in the working year. (For example, a salaried worker earning $24,000 a year and paid monthly would have a gross wage of $2,000 for the pay period.)

In some types of businesses, such as automobile sales or real estate, sales personnel are paid commissions as all or part of their compensation. Computation of commission is not addressed here; however, the computation of deductions from gross wages would be the same as described in this chapter.

PAYROLL DEDUCTIONS

All business firms with employees are required by law to deduct certain state, federal, and (sometimes) local taxes and to remit these taxes directly to the government. Union dues may also have to be deducted and accounted for. In addition, deductions may be made for insurance and other items for which the employee pays in whole or in part. *Net wages* are the amount of wages remaining after all deductions have been taken.

Taxes Withheld from the Employee

Federal and state income taxes and local wage taxes (if any) are withheld from the employee's pay and remitted directly to the appropriate government agency.

Federal Wage Tax and Social Security (FICA)

On printed payroll forms, federal income tax appears as FWT (federal wage tax). What is more commonly called social security appears as FICA (Federal Insurance Contributions Act). The employer must contribute an amount equal to the employees for FICA. This is discussed under "Taxes and Benefits Paid by the Employer." The rates for tax withholdings and employer contributions change yearly. The Internal Revenue Service (IRS) can supply the current rates.

State and Local Income and Wage Taxes

State and local income taxes are similarly deducted from the employee's pay. If the appropriate rate schedules and forms are not available, the employer must secure them.

Unemployment and Disability Taxes

In some states, a portion of the unemployment tax must be withheld from employees. In other states, unemployment taxes are solely the responsibility of the employer. The same is true of state disability funds.

Retirement Contributions

Individual Retirement Accounts (IRAs)

An *individual retirement account* (IRA) is an investment plan that enables an individual to save a part of his or her income for retirement. A traditional IRA allows an individual or a married couple to save a portion of their annual income tax deferred. *Tax-deferred contributions* are not taxed when deposited, but the original amount deposited and the income from the interest earned are taxed when withdrawn. In a *Roth IRA* earnings grow tax free and the proceeds are tax free when withdrawn, but the original contribution does not allow for a tax deduction when deposited. A *simple IRA* is an investment plan that allows employees of small businesses that have fewer than 100 employees to take part in IRAs and save more money per year than with a traditional IRA.

401(k) Plan

A *401(k) plan* is a retirement savings plan that allows an individual to deposit pre-tax dollars from earnings to grow tax free until the money is withdrawn and taxed as regular income. Very often, employers match a part of the individual's contribution into a 401(k).

TAXES AND BENEFITS PAID BY THE EMPLOYER

As already stated, employers must contribute an equal percentage of their employees' FICA (Social Security) taxes; that is, if the current withholding rate is 7.0 percent, the employer must remit an additional 7.0 percent, for a total of 14 percent of employee wages and salaries. Employers must pay state unemployment taxes in whole or in part, depending on the state, and they are liable for federal unemployment taxes if they employ more than a specified number of people. Workers' compensation insurance must also be paid on the basis of payroll (number of employees), either to the state or to a private insurer, depending on state regulations.

In addition, health and dental insurance and other fringe benefits may be payroll related, with or without the employees contributing from their pay.

REPORTING WAGES AND TAX WITHHOLDING

Federal taxes withheld from employees must be reported at least quarterly. Firms with a large number of employees may be required to report monthly or even weekly. Checks for the amounts withheld, plus employer contributions, are drawn and sent at that time. In January, employees receive Form W-2 showing their wages and withholdings for the preceding calendar year.

State and local reporting requirements vary; however, copies of Form W-2 are sent to state taxing agencies in states that have an income tax.

MAINTAINING PAYROLL RECORDS

The Individual Earnings Record

An *individual earnings record* is a record that facilitates the completion of quarterly and annual reports to various taxing agencies. It enables the employer to send out Form W-2s at year-end to all persons employed during the year. An individual earnings record is established for each employee. This form states the employee's wages and the FWT, FICA, and state income taxes withheld; it must be filed with an individual's income tax return.

The Payroll Register

In addition to individual records, a payroll register for the entire firm is prepared for each payroll period, sometimes weekly (Figure 15.1). The *payroll register* lists the names of employees, their hours worked, straight and overtime pay, gross pay, itemized deductions, and net pay. The individual columns are totaled and used to prepare journal entries. The total of the net pay column should equal the total of all paychecks for that period.

The Employee's Individual Payroll Report

An *employee's individual payroll report* is a form that the employee receives with each paycheck showing gross earnings for the pay period, itemizing amounts withheld, and showing net wages. Printed forms for this purpose can be purchased from a stationer. Voucher-style checks incorporating payroll information may also be purchased.

Name	Week Ending:																	Cumulative Totals		
	Hours							Total	Rate	Earnings			Total	Deductions			Net Pay	Deductions		
	Sun	Mon	Tue	Wed	Thu	Fri	Sat	Hours		Reg	Over	Othr	Wages	Social Security	US With. Tax	State With. Tax		Social Security	US With. Tax	State With. Tax

Figure 15.1

ENTERING PAYROLL INFORMATION ON THE BOOKS

Gross pay must be recognized as a business expense. The journal entries shown in Figure 15.2 are made as required, with the payroll register as the source of the information.

Taxes and other withholdings are credited to the appropriate accounts to establish them as liabilities. When they are paid, the appropriate accounts will be debited. (See Figure 15.3.)

Date 20			Dr.	Cr.
Jun.	30	Office Salaries Exp.	$2800	
		Office Salaries Pay.		$2800
	30	Sales Salaries Exp.	3500	
		Sales Salaries Pay.		3500
	30	Wage Expense	950	
		Wage Payable		950
		June's Salaries		
		and wages		

Figure 15.2

Date 20			Dr.	Cr.
Jun.	30	Payroll Tax Expense	$1825	
		FICA Payable		$1030
		Fed. Income Tax Pay.		580
		State Income Tax Pay.		215
Jul.	15	FICA Payable	1030	
		Federal Income Tax Pay.	580	
		State Income Tax Pay.	215	
		Payroll Tax Exp.		1825

Figure 15.3

Additional accounts for such items as payroll-related insurance may be needed as well. These deductions vary too widely to be discussed here.

When all these records are complete, payroll checks may be written or printed. Today, many firms hire services that use computers to maintain payroll records, make out checks, or use direct deposit technology to place the employees' earnings directly into their bank accounts. For those which do not, individual computer programs that calculate taxes, debit and credit the appropriate account, as well as print checks are available. (See Chapter 18.)

SUMMARY

In this chapter you learned something that everyone will agree is important: taking care of paychecks. Several different items that require special attention are federal, state, and local tax rates. Reporting regulations are constantly changing. The firm's owners, or the bookkeeper, should make sure that the appropriate agencies are contacted for information before payroll procedures are set. This will help avoid most problems affecting employees' paychecks. The term gross wages refers to the employee's compensation for the pay period before deduction of taxes or any benefits paid for by the employee. Also discussed were the types of payroll deductions a business may encounter and how to document them properly. These deductions included taxes, insurance, union dues, and various retirement plans. Each business varies, but all have similar reporting and record-keeping requirements.

CHAPTER 16

PARTNERSHIPS

KEY TERMS

partnership, goodwill

Throughout the book, bookkeeping has been discussed in terms of a proprietorship, a one-owner business in which all profits go to a single individual and only one drawing account is used. A *partnership* is a form of business in which two or more persons invest their owner's equity, undertaking a "joint and several" liability (risk) and sharing the profits.

Most bookkeeping for a partnership is like that for a sole proprietorship. However, two or more owner's equity accounts must be set up to show the ownership equity of each partner, arrangements must be made to distribute the profits, and provision may have to be made for additional partners to join the business.

OWNER'S EQUITY ACCOUNTS

With two persons in the partnership, two owner's equity accounts would be set up in the ledger. For example, "John Doe, owner's equity" and "Mary Smith, owner's equity." Similar accounts would be set up for new partners entering the business. As the partnership expands, new owner's equity accounts are set up showing the investment of new partners.

TRANSFERS OF INTEREST

When a new partner buys into a firm, one or all of the existing partners might sell the newcomer a portion of his or her interest in the business. In this case, the seller of an interest keeps the money paid for it, and the owners' equity of the business remains the same as before. An entry might be made in the books to record the transfer of interest. The journal might read: "Rick Smith sold Phil Woods half interest in the business for $125,000." A *debit* in this amount would be posted to the general account. The entry to record the new partner's interest might read: "Phil Woods received half interest in Rick Smith's owner's equity." A *credit* of $250,000 would be posted to the general account.

GOODWILL

Goodwill is an intangible asset a business gains as it establishes a reputation in the community for reliability and good service. This value is added to the tangible assets such as land, equipment, or fixtures to determine the value of a business. When a new partner enters the business, he or she may be charged a price for this goodwill, which may be a few thousand dollars, as in our example, or over a billion dollars for some large corporations. Goodwill is an interesting concept and may be a little difficult to understand at first. Simply put, goodwill is what will cause a consumer to be willing to wait a little longer, or pay a little

20__		Journal	Dr.	Cr.
Aug.	15	Cash	$125,000	
		Goodwill	25,000	
		R. Smith, Owner's Equity		$150,000

Figure 16.1

more, for a product or service. The same can be said for someone buying into a business. She may be willing to pay *more* than half of the book value of the business to become a half owner in the business. That amount of money over the book value would be goodwill. A memorandum journal entry might *debit* cash and *credit* the existing partners' owners' equity accounts: "To credit Rick Smith's owner's equity account with goodwill upon admission of Phil Woods as partner." The journal entry would look like Figure 16.1.

DRAWING ACCOUNTS

If it is agreed that the partners will draw a salary, this withdrawal of cash would be treated as an operating expense to the business and would *debit* salary expense. Other removal of cash for personal use would be shown as a *credit* to the cash account and a *debit* to the partner's drawing account, just as it would for a proprietorship. Drawing accounts are discussed in Chapter 8.

DISTRIBUTING PARTNERSHIP PROFITS

Sometimes profits are distributed equally between or among partners; they are simply divided by the number of partners. Sometimes the partnership agreement calls for distribution of profits in proportion to each partner's investment. Suppose Ms. Smith invested $250,000, Mr. Gross invested $250,000, and Mr. Brown invested $125,000. Smith and Gross would each receive 250,000/625,000 (40 percent) of the profits, and Brown would receive 125,000/625,000 (20 percent).

THE BALANCE SHEET FOR A PARTNERSHIP

The balance sheet for a partnership resembles that for a proprietorship. The only difference is that in the owners' equity section, each owner's equity is shown separately, as found in Figure 16.2.

Balance Sheet

Owners' Equity		
M. Smith	$250,000	
J. Gross	250,000	
P. Brown	125,000	
Total Owners' Equity		$625,000

Figure 16.2

SUMMARY

Most bookkeeping for a partnership is like that for a sole proprietorship. The major differences are that two or more owner's equity accounts must be set up to show the ownership equity of each partner, arrangements must be made to distribute the profits, and a provision may have to be made for additional partners to join the business. Obviously, if there is more than one owner, one would also have to set up more than one owner's drawing account. Each owner is entitled to take his or her share of the profits, so we learned how this is established in the partnership agreement. You also were introduced to the concept of goodwill, an intangible asset a business gains as it establishes a reputation for reliability and good service in the community. This intangible asset is carried on the balance sheet the same as if it were real property. The balance sheet is similar to that of a sole proprietor, except there is an owner's equity account and drawing account for each owner of the partnership.

CHAPTER 17 CORPORATIONS

KEY TERMS

corporation, stockholder, shareholder, dividends, retained earnings, par value, conventional (C) corporation, S corporation, limited liability company (LLC), common stock, preferred stock, treasury stock, equity per share

In the United States, the corporation is the second most popular form of business ownership—behind sole proprietorships and ahead of partnerships. The purpose of this chapter is to familiarize you with the terminology used in corporations. The material here will assist you if you land a bookkeeping job for a corporation. This should also help you in making a decision as to what form of ownership would suit your needs if you decide to start your own business.

WHAT IS A CORPORATION?

A *corporation* is a legal entity created to separate the assets and liabilities of the business from the personal assets and liabilities of its owners among others. Business corporations are formed for profit, although nonprofit corporations also exist for charitable, religious, and philanthropic endeavors.

The owners of a corporation are called stockholders or shareholders. A *stockholder* or *shareholder* is the name given to an individual or another business that owns a portion of a company; that ownership takes the form of shares of stock. A corporation may be owned by an individual, a family, by a few individuals, or by many members of the general public. Generally, a corporation's profit is used two ways: dividends and retained earnings. *Dividends* are the portion of the corporation's profits that are paid out to stockholders. *Retained earnings* are any parts of the profits that are kept and reinvested in the business.

Stock may be used to start the business, or later to raise additional money for expansion or other purposes. It is issued in the form of certificates, which may, if the corporation is publicly held, be sold and resold by their owners or those representing them. *Par value* is the face value of a stock certificate, that is, the price for which it was issued to its original purchasers. It may also be known simply as "par."

As a legal entity, a corporation can do anything an individual owner can do: own property, buy, sell, manufacture, be a party to contracts, sue or be sued, and (of course) be taxed.

TYPES OF CORPORATIONS

There are three different classifications of corporations that will be discussed here. This section will cover some highlights for each form of corporation and their major advantages and disadvantages.

Conventional (C) Corporation

A *conventional (C) corporation* is the most common type of corporation and is typically thought of when discussing corporations. A C corporation may be privately held or publicly traded and enables many people to share the ownership of a business without working there. From this type of corporation, the other forms of corporations originated.

S Corporation

An *S corporation* is a business entity that looks like a corporation but is taxed like a sole proprietorship or a partnership. An S corporation has paperwork requirements that are similar to a C corporation. Profits are taxed as personal income of the stockholders. There are some disadvantages though. An S corporation can have no more than 75 shareholders (150 if you count spouses). All shareholders must be U.S. citizens or permanent residents of the United States. There can only be one class of stock (more on this soon). Finally, no more than 25 percent of the corporation's revenue can come from passive sources, such as rent or royalties.

Limited Liability Company (LLC)

A *limited liability company* (LLC) is similar to an S corporation without the specific eligibility requirements. This relatively new form of business first appeared in 1977. Now, about 15 percent of all new corporations are forming as LLCs. There are several advantages associated with LLCs. Their ownership rules and distribution of profits and losses are flexible. You have a choice in deciding the way the LLC will be taxed—as a partnership or as a corporation. There is no requirement for annual meetings or the recording of minutes. Disadvantages include the fact that there is no stock; you must obtain permission from all members to sell your share of interest in the LLC. LLCs are limited in duration, usually to no more than thirty years. Owners must pay self-employment taxes on all profits of the business, not just on the salary drawn.

TYPES OF CORPORATE STOCK

Corporate bookkeeping can be extremely complex and must be performed by, or at least reviewed by, certified public accountants. Corporations that sell their stock to the public are subject to many state and federal laws. No attempt is made here to describe the complexities of corporate bookkeeping; however, it is useful for bookkeepers to know at least the types of stock that corporations issue.

A number of kinds of stock may be issued. A major difference among types of stock is whether or not they convey voting rights to their owners, which are a say in how the business is run.

- *Common stock* carries voting rights and its owners share equally in any dividends that are distributed.
- *Preferred stock* gives its owners the right to receive their dividends first if the corporation does not earn enough money to pay dividends to all stockholders.
- *Preferred participating stock* provides its holders with the possibility of receiving dividends in excess of a specified amount.
- *Preferred nonparticipating stock* means that dividends paid to holders are limited to a specified amount.

- *Cumulative preferred stock* means that owners receive payment for any prior years' dividends that were missed before other stockholders receive their payments.

- *Noncumulative preferred stock* does not carry the privilege of receiving payment for prior years' dividends that were not distributed.

TREASURY STOCK

On occasion, a corporation may repurchase (buy back) stock that it had previously issued. *Treasury stock* is a firm's own stock that is being held. A company is not permitted to own part of itself, and treasury stock carries no voting rights or dividends. Treasury stock is not an asset; it is a reduction of outstanding shares of the corporation's stock.

EQUITY PER SHARE

One item on the balance sheet or annual report of a corporation of concern to stockholders is the equity per share. This is not the par value of the stock or its value in the stock market. *Equity per share* represents the owner's equity, or the business divided by the number of shares outstanding. Thus, if the owner's equity were $500,000 and 50,000 shares of stock were outstanding, the equity per share would be $500,000/50,000 or $10 a share.

SUMMARY

A corporation is a legal entity created to separate the assets and liabilities of the business from the personal assets and liabilities of its owners. This separation gives the owners protection in the event that the business fails. The owners of a corporation are stockholders and can also be called shareholders. There are several different types of stock available for the corporation. The particular types of stocks a corporation will have for its owners will depend upon the form of corporation chosen when the business was incorporated. The major classifications of corporations were described along with some advantages and disadvantages for each.

The company may pay its owners (shareholders) through dividends, which is the portion of the corporation's profits that is paid out to stockholders. The company may decide to keep some of the profits to be reinvested into the business; this is known as retained earnings. Equity per share represents the owner's equity of the business divided by the number of shares outstanding. Par value is the face value of a stock certificate, that is, the price for which it was issued to its original purchasers, and it may also be known simply as "par."

CHAPTER 18

BOOKKEEPING AND THE COMPUTER

KEY TERMS

software, Internet, spreadsheet program, template, cell, cursor

As computers become less expensive, more powerful, and easier to use, they are taking over some of the more tedious tasks of the bookkeeper in even the smallest businesses. A vast variety of software is available to handle bookkeeping tasks. *Software* is a term used to describe computer programs that control the operations of the computer. Some software programs are designed for small "one-person shops," others for larger firms, and many for specialized types of businesses such as law or contracting firms.

Computer technology changes so fast that even monthly magazines find it difficult to keep up; therefore, it is not practical to give precise instructions for computer bookkeeping in a book. Instead, this chapter gives an overview of the capabilities of certain types of programs and a brief introduction to how they are used.

A MINI-GLOSSARY OF COMPUTER TERMS

- **CD-ROM**—compact disk-read only memory—is a compact disk that can store 700 megabytes of data. Information cannot be written over once it has been written on the disk.
- **CD-RW**—compact disk-rewritable—is like a CD-ROM, but the surface of the disk allows data to be written over the top of old data.
- **Floppies**—magnetized plastic disks 3.5 inches in diameter—are where data and programs are stored.
- **Hardware**—the equipment itself—is the central processing unit (CPU), monitor, keyboard, disk drives.
- **PCs**—microcomputers of the kind used by most small businesses—the term comes from "personal computer."
- **RAM**—random access memory—is the measure of the amount of data a computer can address at any one time. Typically stated in megabytes as 1.2M or gigabytes.
- **ROM**—read only memory—is the internal "memory" that the computer uses to run the software.
- **Software**—the "programs" through which the computer actually operates—virtually all programs used in business. Software is purchased rather than created by the user.

- **Spreadsheet**—a program that permits the user to enter and manipulate many columns of data by equations set up by the user.

CAPABILITIES OF THE COMPUTER

A computer can speed up many bookkeeping operations once a program has been set up with the basic accounts. However, its calculations will only be as accurate as the information its human operator provides.

When combined with a printer, a computer with graphics capability can turn profit and loss information and business plans into charts and graphs. It can instantly update inventory or accounts payable; print checks while automatically updating the appropriate accounts; put information into alphabetical, chronological, or numerical sequence; calculate interest or compare payment terms at different interest rates of maturities; and many similar tasks.

Suppose you wanted to compare the effect of depreciation on profits and taxes using the sum-of-the-years-digits method versus the straight-line method. By changing a few figures you could have the result instantly, on the screen or printed out. With an Internet connection you can transmit information via telephone lines, cable, or other technology to other computers throughout the world. The *Internet* is a network that makes it possible to connect one computer to nearly every other computer in the world.

In your most important bookkeeping responsibilities—preparation of the financial statements used in budgeting and planning—a type of program called a spreadsheet can be invaluable.

A BOOKKEEPER'S OPTIONS

Spreadsheet Programs

A *spreadsheet program* is designed to manipulate data entered into rows and columns. The earliest spreadsheet programs, VisiCalc (1981) and Lotus 1-2-3 (1983), greatly speeded up bookkeeping operations, but data entry was difficult with the original programs. Spreadsheets have come a long way since then. At present, Microsoft Excel is the most widely used spreadsheet program. There are numerous templates that can be obtained to make bookkeeping easier. A *template* is a preformed pattern that saves you a great deal of setup time. For example, you can download an income statement template directly into Excel. Then all you need to do is enter the appropriate data (company name, the particular accounts and their balances) and the template will conduct all of the calculations and display the information in a properly formatted income statement. The income statement can be printed and stored in the computer for later use. Spreadsheet programs are continually being updated by their manufacturers, with more and more features being added to create "integrated software" that incorporates word processing and the management of databases that facilitate keeping and updating inventories of goods for sale and supplies.

With a spreadsheet program, the "framework" of rows and columns appears on the screen. Individual locations in the rows and columns are called cells. A *cell* is a specific point on a spreadsheet defined by the column and row that it occupies. Columns run from top to

Column

Row	A	B	C	D	E	F
1						
2						
3						
4						
5						

Figure 18.1

bottom and may be labeled A, B, C, and so on. Rows run from left to right and may be labeled 1, 2, 3, and so on (see Figure 18.1). You may label columns to store words, some to store numerical entries, some to store results of calculations. The data in the cells can be manipulated with formulas so you can simply input figures and allow the spreadsheet to do all the work for you. For example, columns can be totaled, as needed, to show quarterly or yearly totals. Rows may also be totaled and subtotaled. Various rows and columns may be multiplied, divided, and otherwise manipulated as required by the function you are performing. The results of these operations can be imported into another cell for further manipulation.

To use the program, begin by "defining" or labeling the rows and columns. Then instruct the computer regarding what calculation or equation it is to perform with the rows and columns. For example, you may tell it that the data in Row 1 should be added by the formula D1 = A1 + B1 + C1. In this case, the cell defined by the coordinates (D, 1) will display the sum of the contents in cells A1, B1, and C1. These formulas can be permanently stored so that the program will use them each time.

Your next step is to enter the appropriate data into the individual cells. To do this, you move the cursor. The *cursor* is the symbol that shows you "where the mouse is pointing" and indicates where data from the keyboard or other input device will go. Figure 18.2 shows a simple setup that will compute operating expenses by type (the rows) and period incurred (the columns).

Here are the steps used to create Figure 18.2 in Microsoft Excel:

1. Open Microsoft Excel on your computer.

2. Use your mouse to point at cell A1 (top left cell), then click (depress the left button on the mouse) to select it.

A	A	B	C	D	E	F
1	Utilities Account		January	February	March	1st Quarter
2	Electric		245	220	197	662
3	Gas		178	162	115	455
4	Water		42	50	47	139
5	Telephone		231	286	270	787
6	Internet		75	75	75	225
7	Total		771	793	704	2268

Figure 18.2

3. Type in the words "Utilities Account," then press Enter.

4. The curser should be in cell A2 now. Type in the word "Electric," then press Enter. (See Figure 18.2.)

5. The curser should be in cell A3 now. Continue typing in the words in the utilities account, one at a time, repeating steps 3 and 4 until you have entered the word "Total."

6. Now let's label the months. Select cell C1 (by left clicking) and enter January. Continue entering the months and the "1st Quarter" title into cells D1, E1, and F1 as we did for the accounts above, with one exception. Instead of depressing the enter key after typing in the data, we will now press the Tab Key. This will cause the cursor to move to the next cell to the right. If we had pressed enter before, no big deal! You can simply click in the appropriate cell using the mouse.

7. Now that our table is labeled, we can start to enter data. Enter the data from Figure 18.2 for each of the categories. This will be entered just like the other information was entered. Simply type the number for the particular cell you are in and Enter (to go down), or Tab (to go the right), or use the mouse to point and click on the cell you want to move to. Do not put the totals in, though!

8. Now we want to start letting the spreadsheet work for us! We want to have the columns totaled, so we know how much we spent on utilities each month. Here is where the computer starts to help us. We will select all the cells from C2 down to C7 by clicking on cell C2 and dragging (keep the left mouse button depressed as you move the mouse down the screen) down to cell C7. Release the mouse button. All of those cells are shaded a different color now. Here comes the best part. Click on the symbol that looks like Σ on the toolbar. That is the auto sum symbol. It adds up all the numbers and displays the answer in the last cell of the highlighted group.

9. To get the sum of the other columns, we can copy the formula we just created into the other cells across from the total label. Momentarily depress the right mouse button while pointing at cell C7 (this is known as a right-click). You will notice that a small window has appeared to the right of the curser. Select the copy function by moving the pointer over the copy symbol in the pop-up window and click (left mouse button).

10. Now select cells D7 though F7 (similar to step 8 above) by dragging across from D7 to F7 with the left button depressed. Release the mouse button, then right-click, and the pop-up window appears again. Select paste by clicking on the word or symbol in the pop-up. And as Emeril Lagasse says, "Bam!" You now have totals in all of the columns except for the first quarter's total.

11. To get totals for each of the utilities, we will use the auto sum feature again. Click and drag across from C2 to F2, then click on the auto sum icon, Σ. This will provide your total for electricity in the first quarter. Now we will copy that formula into the remaining utilities cells. Right-click on the F2 cell, select copy, select cells F3 to F6 by dragging across them, then right-click and select paste. Now you have totals for each individual utility for the quarter.

This simple sheet can be used to answer many different questions. We can readily determine how much we spent on electricity each month and for the quarter. We can see how much we spent on all utilities for each individual month as well as for the entire quarter. This can be easily expanded to cover more information. Suppose the telephone fees are from three different sources: local business phone line, long-distance provider, and mobile phone service. We would want to track each of these expenses separately. We can do this using the same spreadsheet we just created.

Here is how to create a miniature worksheet using Excel:

1. Click on cell A12 and type in an appropriate label for the miniature work sheet (I chose telephone work sheet).

2. In cells A13 though A16 type Mobile (A13), Office Phone (A14), Long Distance (A15), and Total (A16).

3. In cell C13 enter the amount of the January mobile phone bill, $76.

4. Continue entering the data from Figure 18.3. Do not enter the totals though.

5. Now let's set up the auto sum formula. Select C13 through C16 and click on the auto sum icon. Now we will copy that formula into cells D16 through F16. Using the same technique we used in step 9 that we used earlier, select C16, then right-click C16, then select Copy. We can also set up the quarterly total using the auto sum function. Select C13 through F13, then auto sum. Copy that formula from C13 into C14 and C15.

We can now modify our original utilities account spreadsheet. There is no reason for us to have the computer add the data and not have it install or import it into the appropriate cell above. Simply select C5 (January's telephone expense cell) press the = key, then

A	A	B	C	D	E	F
1	Utilities Account		January	February	March	1st Qtr.
2	Electric		245	220	197	662
3	Gas		178	162	115	455
4	Water		42	50	47	139
5	Telephone		231	286	270	787
6	Internet		75	75	75	225
7	Total		771	793	704	2268
8						
9						
10						
11						
12	Telephone Worksheet					
13	Mobile		76	86	85	247
14	Office Phone		125	125	125	375
15	Long Distance		30	75	60	165
16	Total		231	286	270	787

Figure 18.3

click in cell C16 (total of telephone charges from the worksheet), and finally press Enter. You will see that the amount matches. We will want to copy that rule into the other telephone cells. This is also very easy. Simply click on cell C5, then right-click, select Copy, and drag across to cell E5, right-click, then select Paste. The computer automatically chooses data from the correct cell and places it in these cells. Now if we change something in the worksheet, that change will be reflected in the utilities account as well. For example, we recorded $86 for the February mobile phone charge. We transposed the numbers when we typed it in; it should have been $68. If we go into the worksheet and change the 86 to 68, we will see the total change from 286 to 268 on the worksheet. This would be reflected in the utilities account as well. The total utilities expense for February will change from 793 to 775 and the telephone expense for the quarter will change from 787 to 769. The utilities quarterly expense total will change from 2,268 to 2,250. All of these changes occur painlessly after we have built the framework for the spreadsheet.

I am going to go one step further. We have this spreadsheet set up for one quarter's information. Look at how simple it is to make it ready for a second quarter. First, label cells G1 through J1 with April, May, June, and 2nd Quarter. Second, click on cell C2 and drag across to F2 and down to F16. Then right-click and select Copy. Finally, click on cell G2 and drag across to J2 and down to J16, then right-click and select Paste. Now all of the data and formulas have been transferred into another quarter. All that remains is to put in the appropriate data. For aesthetic reasons you may want to delete the first quarter information from the second quarter cells. Do this by simply clicking on G2 and dragging down to I4, then press Delete. Then click on G6 and drag over to I6 and press Delete. We did not delete the entire box because the formulas would have been deleted as well. We do the same for the worksheet we built for the telephone account. Simply select and delete the contents of cells G13 to I15.

Figure 18.4 shows all of these changes and should match yours if you were able to work along with the text.

A	A	B	C	D	E	F	G	H	I	J
1	Utilities Account		January	February	March	1st Qtr.	April	May	June	2nd Qtr.
2	Electric		245	220	197	662				
3	Gas		178	162	115	455				
4	Water		42	50	47	139				
5	Telephone		231	268	270	769	0	0	0	0
6	Internet		75	75	75	225				
7	Total		771	775	704	2250	0	0	0	0
8										
9										
10										
11										
12	Telephone Worksheet									
13	Mobile		76	68	85	229				
14	Office Phone		125	125	125	375				
15	Long Distance		30	75	60	165				
16	Total		231	268	270	769	0	0	0	0

Figure 18.4

These are very simple examples. A more complex spreadsheet might show depreciation schedules for hundreds of items of equipment. Or it might contain current and projected operating statements, with each item on the statement (revenues, cost of goods sold, individual operating expenses, gross and net profits) in a column and the years of operation in rows. By changing a single figure, say increasing revenue by 20 percent or taxes by 50 percent, you could project the effect on net income or profit for the current year and all ensuing years. You could then print out this information for comparison with a different projection.

Complex spreadsheets with many columns cannot be viewed on the screen all at once. However, they may be "scrolled" sideways or up and down on the screen. Programs offer "windows" by which a chosen portion of the spreadsheet may be superimposed on a part of the screen.

Spreadsheet programs are complex and sometimes difficult to learn. Once mastered, however, they more than repay the effort involved. Computer vendors generally offer a certain amount of training with the purchase price and community colleges and private institutions offer courses on the more popular programs.

Accounting Programs

There are numerous accounting programs available for use by bookkeepers. Prices range from a few dollars (less than $50) to many thousands of dollars for a program that is custom tailored to the business's exact needs. Most needs of a bookkeeping operation can be fulfilled with several programs in the $50 to $500 range. There are also programs that can cost tens of thousands of dollars and do just about everything!

We will focus on the programs that most small businesses can afford. The two most dominant bookkeeping/accounting programs are Peachtree® Software and QuickBooks®. Both programs offer a very useful package starting around $100. Each has several packages available with prices that are nearly identical, with the top of the line off-the-shelf product priced around $500. QuickBooks offers industry-specific software in its Premier edition. Peachtree provides a more concrete audit trail. Both products offer a 60-day return policy.

MAKING CORRECTIONS IN COMPUTERIZED BOOKKEEPING

The rules for making changes are the same whether you are using paper or a computer. There should be evidence and a reason for the change. Some computer programs will allow you to change a previously closed set of books. That may be okay if you trust your bookkeeper or are doing the books yourself. Either way, you should document the change by making a journal entry. You are never wrong if you provide written evidence, or a trail, to show why the change was made and how the error occurred and was discovered.

SUMMARY

Nearly every business today uses a computer to assist in bookkeeping, so learning about the capabilities of computers is very important. This chapter discussed some of the terminology you may encounter while using computers, as well as some of the different ways computers can assist with bookkeeping tasks. One of the most common is through the use of spreadsheets. Spreadsheets can be created and used alone or they may be found in sophisticated accounting programs. In this chapter you learned the step-by-step procedure through the creation of a simple spreadsheet program to account for utilities expenses. You also learned how easy it is to "Copy and Paste" information, in this case to duplicate the formulas that were used in the first quarter, the second quarter, and so on. This allows you to input the particular data for the subsequent quarters without having to regenerate the formulas. In other words, you can focus on bookkeeping and let the computer do the math.

This chapter also introduced you to the two most popular bookkeeping/accounting programs, Peachtree and QuickBooks. These two programs are inexpensive and very functional. Additionally, there are other programs that can be purchased with prices anywhere between a few dollars to tens of thousands of dollars. One thing that remains constant in all forms of bookkeeping is that mistakes can happen. When they do, the errors must be corrected and documented in journal entries, which was discussed earlier in this book.

GLOSSARY

401(k) plan
A retirement savings plan that allows an individual to deposit pre-tax dollars. The earnings grow tax free until the money is withdrawn, upon which it is taxed as regular income.

accelerated depreciation
When the greatest proportion of the expense is taken in the first year, with successively smaller amounts being taken in later years.

account
Where journal entries are transferred and recorded.

accounts receivable
Money owed by customers of the business for goods or services they have purchased on credit.

adjusted trial balance
Balance at the end of an accounting period (usually one year) that reflects changes not previously recorded in day-to-day accounting.

adjustments to journal entries
Method of ensuring that all changes in the business are recorded in the journal.

asset
Any property the business owns, and any claim it has on the property of others.

balance sheet
Shows what the business owns (assets), what it owes (liabilities), and what the owners would have left if the business paid everything it owes out of everything it owns (owner's equity).

bank reconciliation
Prepared to verify the accuracy of the bank's records and the firm's checking account register.

bank statement
Indicates all activity in a bank account for the month.

book of original entry
Another name for the journal. It is the starting place for all bookkeeping.

book value
Current depreciated value of an asset (or of all assets except land). It is determined by subtracting its accumulated depreciation from its cost.

business
Consists of all commercial activities designed to sell goods and services to customers at a profit.

capital
See owner's equity.

capital asset
Permanent item used directly or indirectly to produce the product or service the business sells such as a warehouse, a truck, a milling machine, or a computer.

cell
Specific point on a spreadsheet defined by the column and row that it occupies.

chart of accounts
Single index page that is kept to list all the account titles used in daily bookkeeping operations along with their numbers.

check register
Running record of all checks written, deposits made, interest earned, and bank charges or fees imposed on a checking account.

close the books
Ready each revenue and expense account for the next accounting period, to adjust the owner's equity account by the amount of the profit or loss incurred in the previous period, and to reflect money drawn by the owner for personal use.

common stock
Carries voting rights and its owners share equally in any dividends that are distributed.

compound entries
Made when a transaction affects more than two accounts.

contra asset
An account that is charged against an asset.

controlling accounts
One-page summaries of subsidiary accounts, such as the accounts receivable summary account and the accounts payable summary account.

conventional (C) corporation
Most common type of corporation.

corporation
Legal entity created to separate the assets and liabilities of the business from the personal assets and liabilities of its owners.

cost of goods sold
Total cost to manufacture or procure items that were sold at retail.

credit
Always entered in the right-hand column of a T-account.

credit terms
Terms under which a firm sells to its open account (charge) customers. This is also known as the terms of sale.

cross-referencing
Name given for the practice of using notes in journals and ledgers that show where the entries came from.

cumulative preferred stock
Owners receive payment for any prior years' dividends that were missed before other stockholders receive their payments.

current asset
Cash or items that will become cash in the foreseeable future because they are intended for sale or items the business will consume within one year.

current liabilities
What a company currently owes its suppliers and creditors.

cursor
Symbol that shows you where the computer mouse is pointing and indicates where data from the keyboard or other input device will go.

debit
Always entered in the left-hand column of a T-account.

depreciation
Reduction in value of an asset as it is used.

discounted note
Loan in which the interest on the note is paid in advance.

dividends
Portions of the corporation's profits that are paid out to stockholders.

double declining balance method
Accelerated method of depreciation when the residual (salvage) value is ignored until the end. The percentage of depreciation taken each year is based on the straight-line rate multiplied by two.

double-entry system
Each transaction is recorded twice, as a credit to one account and a debit to another.

drawee
Bank on which the face amount (the sum for which the check is written) is drawn.

drawer
Person or business that creates the check and signs it on its face (the front).

drawing account
Ledger account where money that the owner has withdrawn for his or her personal use is recorded.

employee's individual payroll report
Form that the employee receives with each paycheck showing gross earnings for the pay period, itemizing amounts withheld, and showing net wages.

entry
Term used to describe the recording of a transaction.

equity
Any debt a business owes.

equity per share
Represents the owner's equity of the business divided by the number of shares outstanding.

expenses
Cost of doing business; they constitute an outflow of assets.

FIFO
First in/first out method of assigning wholesale value to inventory.

fixed assets
Items that are not for sale; they are used in operating the business.

general journal
Daily "diary" in which each transaction is recorded. It is also known as the journal.

goodwill
Intangible asset a business gains as it establishes a reputation in the community for reliability and good service.

gross wages
Total of all wages and overtime before taxes and other deductions have been imposed.

imprest fund
Advanced (loaned) money.

income statement
Lists income over a specified period of time, such as a year or a calendar quarter, and subtracts expenses over the same period to show whether a profit was earned or a loss incurred for that time frame. It is also known as a profit and loss statement, or P&L.

income summary
Account created to summarize the information from all the revenue and expense accounts (and is only used when closing the books). Sometimes called a profit and loss statement (P&L).

individual earnings records
A record that facilitates the completion of quarterly and annual reports to various taxing agencies.

Individual Retirement Account (IRA)
Tax-deferred investment plan that enables an individual to save a part of his or her income for retirement.

initial capital
Money or other assets that the owner puts into the business to meet start-up expenses and keep the business running until money from customers begins to come in.

interest
Rent charged for the use of money.

interest rate
Amount charged for a loan expressed as a percentage.

Internet
Network that makes it possible to connect one computer to nearly any other computer in the world.

inventory
Stock of goods on hand for sale.

journal
Basic tool for recording all transactions.

journal entry
Process of recording transactions that have occurred in the journal; more formally called journalizing.

journalizing
Practice where every time a transaction is made it is recorded.

ledger
Book of accounts in which each individual type of transaction is maintained separately.

ledger T-accounts
Similar to journal T-accounts in that the left column is called the debit (Dr.) side and the right column is called the credit (Cr.) side.

liabilities
Legal claims against the business by persons or corporations other than the owners.

LIFO
Last in/first out method of assigning wholesale value to inventory.

limited liability company (LLC)
Similar to an S corporation without the specific eligibility requirements.

liquidity
Speed that an asset can be turned into cash.

long-term liabilities
Like capital assets.

maturity
Date when the loan comes due.

negotiable instrument
Written promise of one person to pay a specific sum of money to another person either on demand or on a certain date in the future.

net income
What remains after all expenses are subtracted from revenues.

net loss
Term given when total expenses exceed total revenue for a firm.

net wages
Amount of wages remaining after all deductions have been taken.

net worth
See owner's equity.

noncumulative preferred stock
Does not carry the privilege of receiving payment for prior years' dividends that were not distributed.

normal account balance
The side of the account (debit or credit) where increases are recorded.

operating margin
Used as a guide to set pricing and computed by dividing the gross profit on sales by the gross sales.

owner's equity
Amount left over after all liabilities have been deducted from assets; portion of the assets belonging to the owner of the business. Sometimes called capital or net worth.

partnership
Form of business in which two or more persons invest their capital, undertaking a "joint and several" liability (risk) and sharing the profits.

par value
Face value of a stock certificate, that is, the price for which it was issued to its original purchaser; and may also be known as "par."

payee
Person or business that receives a check and must endorse (sign) it on the back to cash or deposit it.

payroll register
Lists the names of employees, their hours worked, straight and overtime pay, gross pay, itemized deductions, and net pay.

petty cash fund
Fund established for the payment of small cash expenses.

petty cash journal
Used to record all transactions to a petty cash fund.

petty cash voucher
Slip or form recording who received the money, the date, and the purpose of the expenditure; it may be signed or initialed by the person responsible for the petty cash fund.

posting
Process of transferring information from journal entries to accounts.

preferred nonparticipating stock
Means that dividends paid to holders are limited to a specified amount.

preferred participating stock
Provides its holders with the possibility of receiving dividends in excess of a specified amount.

preferred stock
Gives its owners the right to receive their dividends first if the corporation does not earn enough money to pay dividends to all stockholders.

principal
Amount of money borrowed.

profit and loss statement (P&L)
See income statement.

promissory note
Written commitment by one person to pay a definite sum of money to another on a specified future date.

purchase journals
Used to record purchases for inventory and other assets purchased on account (credit).

retailers
Firms that buy goods at wholesale and sell them to consumers; they maintain an inventory of goods for sale. Also known as merchandisers.

retained earnings
Any part of the profit that is kept and reinvested in the business.

revenues
Earnings of the business, the money that comes in from the sale of products (sales revenue) or services (service revenue).

Roth IRA
IRA where the earnings grow tax free and the proceeds are tax free when withdrawn, but the original contribution does not allow for a tax deduction when deposited.

S corporation
Business entity that runs like a corporation but is taxed as a sole proprietorship or a partnership.

salaries
Compensation paid to supervisory and management employees who are hired at a flat yearly, monthly, or (sometimes) weekly compensation.

sales allowance
Price reduction given to a customer, for example, because goods are damaged.

sales journal
Used if many sales are made "on account," that is, on credit.

sales organizations
Businesses that sell tangible products to their consumers.

salvage value
Trade-in value or estimated selling price at the end of an asset's useful life.

service organizations
Businesses that provide a service rather than tangible products for their customers.

shareholder
Name given to an individual or another business that owns a portion of a company. That ownership takes the form of shares of stock, also known as stockholder.

simple IRA
Investment plan that allows small businesses with fewer than 100 employees to take part in an IRA and save more money per year than a traditional IRA.

slide error
Occurs when you unintentionally move a number over one decimal place such as writing $10,000 instead of $1,000 or $100,000.

software
Term used to describe computer programs that control the operations of the computer.

special journals
Used to group common types of entries into separate journals, which simplifies the process of making manual journal entries.

spreadsheet program
Designed to manipulate data entered into rows and columns.

stockholder
See shareholder.

straight-line depreciation
Where the salvage value is deducted from the cost and the remaining amount is divided by the estimated useful life of the asset.

subsidiary ledgers
Customer and vendor accounts are kept separate from main ledgers in folders, binders, or computer files.

sum-of-years-digits method
Method of depreciation that uses a calculation where a fraction in which the numerator (top number in a fraction) consists of the remaining years of the expected lifetime and the denominator (bottom number in a fraction) is the sum of all the years of life.

sundry account
Used to record infrequent or unusual transactions that have no column in the special journal.

T-account
Represents a ledger account and is used to see the effects of one or more transactions.

tax-deferred contributions
Contributions are not taxed when deposited, but the original amount deposited and the income from the interest earned are taxed when withdrawn.

template
Preformatted pattern that saves you a great deal of setup time.

time
Number of months or days the principal is held by the borrower.

trade discount
Reduction from the list price of merchandise or a service offered to other businesses that purchase a firm's goods or services.

transaction
Any business dealing that involves money.

transposition error
Occurs when you inadvertently reverse numbers when writing or entering them on a keyboard—for example, recording 67 instead of 76.

treasury stock
Holding of a firm's own stock.

trial balance
List of all accounts and their balances at a specific point in time.

unadjusted trial balance
Trial balance before adjustments are made to correct for unrecorded changes to various accounts during the financial period.

units of production method
Consists of first deducting the salvage value and then dividing the purchase price by the number of units thought to be the best indicator of usefulness (for example, mileage or hours of operation).

wage
Hourly compensation paid for nonmanagement employees.

wholesalers
Organizations that purchase goods directly from the manufacturer and sell them to retailers.

INDEX

D

E

Q

R

S

NOTES